Luca Collins has spent the last twenty years running dramatic storybuilding and creative writing workshops. WRITER is the culmination of all the workshops taught or attended. He is a filmmaker, published playwright, set designer and builder, actor and director. His short film 'First' was screened in two international film festivals. He has a Masters in Creative Writing from the University of Technology, Sydney.

First published by Luca Collins in 2017
This edition published in 2017 by Luca Collins

Copyright © Luca Collins 2017

The moral right of the author has been asserted.

All rights reserved. This publication (or any part of it) may not be reproduced or transmitted, copied, stored, distributed or otherwise made available by any person or entity (including Google, Amazon or similar organisations), in any form (electronic, digital, optical, mechanical) or by any means (photocopying, recording, scanning or otherwise) without prior written permission from the publisher.

Writer: How to write short stories, novellas and novels

EPUB format: 9781925579420
Print on Demand format: 9781925579437

Cover design by Red Tally Studios

Publishing services provided by Critical Mass
www.critmassconsulting.com

CONTENTS

WRITER HOW TO WRITE SHORT STORIES, NOVELLAS AND NOVELS – LUCA COLLINS   1
- PREFACE   5
- INTRODUCTION   9
- CHAPTER ONE – BASIC STRUCTURE   12
- CHAPTER TWO – STORY CONCEPTS IN GENERAL   19
- CHAPTER THREE – FINDING IDEAS TO BEGIN YOUR STORY   32
- CHAPTER FOUR – PEOPLING YOUR STORY   46
- CHAPTER FIVE – DEEPER STORY STRUCTURE   70
- CHAPTER SIX – DEEPER QUESTIONS AND APPROACHES   83
- CHAPTER SEVEN – CREATING WORLDS   111
- CHAPTER EIGHT – BUILDING BLOCKS   119
- CHAPTER NINE – ADDING SUBSTANCE   146
- CHAPTER TEN – STYLISTIC CONSIDERATIONS   168

CONTENTS

CHAPTER ELEVEN – GENERAL HOUSEKEEPING	181
WRITER II. HOW TO WRITE FANTASY FICTION USING THE HERO'S JOURNEY – LUCA COLLINS	**205**
INTRODUCTION	207
CHAPTER ONE – THE BASICS	210
CHAPTER TWO – THE COMMON WORLD AND BEYOND	220
CHAPTER THREE – STEPPING ACROSS	229
CHAPTER FOUR – MEETINGS ON THE ROAD	237
CHAPTER FIVE – DANGER AND DARKNESS	244
CHAPTER SIX – LANDSCAPE OF THE JOURNEY	259
CHAPTER SEVEN – THE FINAL ORDEAL	263
CHAPTER EIGHT – THE PSYCHOLOGY OF THE FINAL ORDEAL	269
CHAPTER NINE – WHAT IS WON AND LOST AND COMING HOME	275
CHAPTER TEN – DEEPER INSIGHTS	282
APPENDIX	312
RECOMMENDED RESOURCES	314

WRITER
How to Write Short Stories, Novellas and Novels
Luca Collins

To my life-long friend Geoff Quick for his critical eye and unswerving loyalty. To Ullas Bell and Vandan Guinness for their friendship and big hearts.

PREFACE

Including a word or two about Copyright and Harry

You want to become a writer but don't know where to start. You read books but don't know how the author creates that magic. In *Writer* the building blocks, the structures and techniques of story creation are covered in detail. *Writer* focuses on character, plot, dialogue, authorial and narrative voice and much more. Here we cover just about all you will want to know, then send you to other sources so that you can extend your knowledge.

But *Writer* requires an open mind. There are references, within this text to books that are considered among the great works of the Western Canon. Some are demanding reads [especially the 17th and 18th century tomes] but the insights they offer are beyond measure. If you want to be a serious author, then make the effort with these works. If you like your reading light, and you avoid the dense and voluminous master works, you will miss much of what the great writers offer.

If you consider only the accepted great writers as worthy, you also will miss much. Let me remind you that the exalted

Charles Dickens was a pulp fiction writer, who produced his work in short instalments in popular magazines.

Science Fiction, Fantasy, Horror, Crime and other members of this motley crew have as much to teach as 'Classic' Literature. We can go anywhere, be anything and create any situation, no matter how much we stretch reality. And there are invaluable lessons to be learnt from these kinds of writings. In fact, many of the 'great classics of the canon' are fantasy fictions. Just ask Jules Verne, Jonathan Swift and Lewis Carroll {Ok they're dead but you get my point}.

So be brave and open and let us see where we end up, hopefully *'There and back again.'*

A WORD ABOUT COPYRIGHT

Much of the source material I have used I cite in the appendix,
However, over the years I have been handed books, photocopied texts, compilations of ideas, individually created lessons, handwritten notes and diagrams and not all of it footnoted. Thank you to all those teachers and mentors who helped me along the way.

I have attempted to find the sources of all material used then and now. If I have not acknowledged you, it was never intentional. Contact me and as Puck says, *'If you pardon we will mend"*

A TOUCH OF HARRY IN THE NIGHT

There are references to many great books and authors in *Writer* but the one that is cited most often is the *'Harry Potter'* series. I make no apology for this, as in terms of fantasy literature it is among the best. And in terms of the contemporary novel J.K.

Rowling has much to teach as well. I do not reference the latest literary sensation, as it is impossible to stay current.

The *'Potter'* books cover a great many of the facets of good fantasy and mainstream fiction that we need to look at. Also, it is the one series that many of the readers of this book are most likely to have read themselves. That alone makes the series indispensable.

Also, it would be helpful if you were familiar with *'The Lord of the Rings'* by J.R.R. Tolkien, *'A Tale of Two Cities'* by Charles Dickens and for Writer II Kate Forsyth's *'Bitter Greens'*. The first two are films if time is an issue, though I do recommend the read; while the latter is a wonderful blend of the fantastic and the realistic. It is a clever example of what you might achieve by blending the knowledge of both Writer I and Writer II. Also for further research within Writer II it will be necessary for you to have watched the fantasy film *'Ladyhawke'* [available for streaming]

INTRODUCTION

Inspiration, Perspiration and Imagination

Like all creative pursuits, writing is a mixture of inspiration and perspiration – ideas plus hard work. Take imagination and natural gifts then add knowledge and experience plus a strong work regime and hopefully produce writing that excites others.

This book is designed to give you the knowledge and techniques that will allow you to write with depth and breadth. When you have the required knowledge, you consolidate it with exercises that reinforce what you have learnt.

While creating stories much happens automatically, for you have a great deal of background knowledge already, having been exposed to stories all your life. Here we focus in on that knowledge then add to and extend.

Newfound knowledge will find its' way into your writing, as you employ techniques and structures that all writers use. Much of this will happen simultaneously. You will start to develop characters, story structure, turning points, story and character arcs and dialogue all in parallel with each other or at least in quick succession. You will jump from one to another as the ideas cascade. What you will learn here is how to set up the concepts and structures that will let a story flow.

The world is made up of stories. Our lives are filled with stories. Stories are one of the attributes of being human. No other animal tells stories.

But what makes a story successful?

To write an effective story we must understand how to build it, how to people it with believable characters who speak believable dialogue, how to put those characters in danger, in confusion, in circumstances that test their courage, compassion and ingenuity.

A WORD OF WARNING

Although there are structures and blueprints for many of the aspects of creative writing we are still talking about **SPONTANIETY.**

THIS BOOK IS ABOUT FORM NOT FORMULA.

It would be a mistake to think if you simply set up all the structures in a formulaic way that you will end up with great writing. Writing is spontaneous but the magic takes many years of refinement. And that refinement comes with a wealth of background knowledge programmed into your creative circuitry. {See **THE A-HA MOMENT, FIRST DRAFT AND SPONTANIETY**}

I tend to write my shorter stories in an organic way, putting down ideas that flow one to another and then I go back. Second drafts include tightening dialogue, correcting grammar and punctuation, removing clichés, fixing plot holes, rearranging sequences within act structures, inverting subject and object within a sentence, weeding out word repetitions and improving character and motivation. But Novellas and Novels need to have more complex structure and development as well as deeper characterisation and more intricate plotting. Then there is the level of research, world creation and backstory. Now spontaneity comes with a great deal of organisation. I feel that to simply begin a larger work at the first word and stop two hundred pages later, without any preparation is not the way to go. Alright it worked for Jack Kerouac but there is only one '*On the Road*' and that's of its time.

CHAPTER ONE
BASIC STRUCTURE

The Three Act Structure
The Ticking Clock
The Five Positions of Story Structure

THE THREE ACT STRUCTURE

Introduction/Orientation/Act One
Development/Complication/Act Two
Conclusion/Resolution/Act Three
Exercise 1.

Stories are, at their simplest, broken up into three parts

Introduction	OR	Orientation
Development		Complication
Conclusion		Resolution

These are the forms and names that have been handed to students throughout the centuries, to help them write stories. Authors have used them over time, knowing them simply as the Three Act Structure. The Three Act Structure goes back to Aristotle and *'The Poetics'*.

Even something as simple as a joke uses this formula. There is the setup, the misdirected middle or complication and the punch line – the pay off.

ACT ONE

INTRODUCTION/ORIENTATION

Orientation is about where you set your story. Important decisions need to be made here. How you design the setting and what you create in that world will open up possibilities for your story. So be imaginative, be thorough, and be cohesive. Create a world that is lived in.

John Steinbeck, Thomas Hardy, Emily Bronte, J.R.R. Tolkien to name but a few, create worlds that have immense detail. They have sound and smell, sight, colour and texture. They are worlds that are complete enough to feel lived in. You recognize them as real.

Later we will look at techniques to build these worlds but for now let us stay with story structure.

ACT TWO

DEVELOPMENT/COMPLICATION

In this act, the characters/heroes/protagonists meet and defeat a number of problems/obstacles. Creating your middle act is one of the most important facets of writing a satisfying story. It is here that friendships are forged and tested, here that a lead character proves their worth, here that fears are revealed and faced. It is also here * **THE TICKING CLOCK** appears.

Within this act, untested skills and character traits are called upon, here human frailty and misunderstanding will undermine the character's progress, here fate or a villain's intentions are magnified into defined menaces. It is here that fate plays a cruel hand and leads to destruction. Or this is where the main character chooses or has forced upon them a road of trials and tribulations.

At this point gifts and knowledge are drawn upon. Many of these are passed on by guides or previous failed survivors. If this is the first in a series, then this is where you lay out much of what is to be revealed later- you are setting up twists and riddles that will have pay offs in the future. We will go into greater detail later {much of it at the other end of the book in WRITER II}, for now we are looking at the overview of structure.

The Climax, the denouement where events, action, danger, fate all come to together at the crucial point will often fall on the cusp of Act II and Act III.

ACT THREE

CONCLUSION/RESOLUTION

This is the act where reasonably quickly and succinctly the author brings the story threads together to form a satisfying ending. Satisfying but that does not always mean a positive and happy ending. In the final act, you are required to put to rest unanswered questions [at least most of them].

Here is where the lessons learnt are evaluated or simply restated. Here is where the main character may take a philosophical approach to the lessons learnt in the preceding narrative. Here is where themes are discussed, illuminated and pondered. But also in smaller just as important detail, you are recognizing and focusing on the strong bonds between central characters. Failures are forgiven and love between them is often celebrated. Also, revelations about the villain's intentions, their deceptions and possibly their long-range plans are clarified in this final act. It is here that surprise revelations occur and ironic twists appear.

In some cases, if this is not a "stand alone" story there may be unanswered questions and unfinished business that must be dealt with in later instalments. If not, this is where you leave your reader with the completed tale.

Again, much of this three-act structure will be explored in tandem with character development, story arc and character arc in later sections.

EXERCISE 1.

A short story is the easiest and quickest way to identify the three acts of Story structure. You can find the Guy de Maupassant short story *'The Necklace'* on the internet at www.eastoftheweb.com

Look at the story and find where it changes and the three acts are apparent. Read the story and identify the acts before reading the following.

Act One begins with a description of the central character; the wife of a lower middle class civil servant. She is a woman who desires a better life and dreams of fine clothes and fancy balls. When her husband procures an invitation to just such a ball she frets until she has bought a beautiful gown and borrowed an expensive necklace. They attend the ball and she is the centre of attention.

Act Two begins with the complication. She has lost the necklace and though they search for hours, making many attempts to find it, the necklace is gone. They borrow to buy a replacement and return an expensive facsimile to its owner. Now a life of poverty and debt stretches before them.

Act Three begins many years later when, beaten down by the hardships she has endured, the wife meets the well to do owner of the necklace on the street. Here a revelation and an ironic twist occur. This kind of ending is often used in short stories. {See Chapter Eleven Short Story Writing.}

*THE TICKING CLOCK

Time is running out for our heroes and what that means to a story

The ticking clock hangs over characters and situations in a story, as it also hangs over our own lives. In a story, it is the idea that the characters must complete a task, in a prescribed time or all is lost. The character[s] need to accomplish the task/solve the mystery/rescue the captive/find the solution/defeat the menace/gain the coveted prize BEFORE three days/the setting of the sun/midnight/their disguise disappears/their subterfuge is uncovered/the real person they are impersonating returns/the bomb explodes/the criminal returns ETC. Of course, it sounds like I am only talking about adventure and fantasy writing but the 'Ticking Clock' is there in mainstream literature too. We are waiting for Big Brother and the Party's Thought Police to discover Winston Smith and Julia's transgressions in '1984'. We know that it is only a matter of time before the authorities come for Tess after she has killed Alec D'Urberville – *'Tess of the D'Urbervilles'*. We know that when Ahab meets the White Whale that he has obsessed over that the meeting will be cataclysmic if not fatal - *'Moby Dick'*.

There are countless versions of the main character-ticking clock dilemma but they all serve the same purpose. That is to *'up the ante'*, to make the moment even more loaded with imminent danger. It is the life and death sentence that we all have, reduced to days, hours and minutes for our reading pleasure.

THE FIVE POSITIONS OF STORYTELLING

Another variant of Story Structure

Sometimes called the Story Arc or Freytag's Triangle this is another way of looking at the basic structure of traditional linear storytelling.

Exposition or Set Up

Here vital information important to the audience is introduced, using dialogue, flashbacks, prologues, preambles, reminiscences or frame narrators. Much of this will be clearer later as we investigate these terms. This, however is the first and last time we will use exposition with this meaning.

Rising Action

This is the series of events that build toward a climax. Here is discovered aspects of character, machinations of foes, relationships and desires, twists and ironies.

Climax

This is the turning point that alters the main character's fate. The point where the protagonist rises or falls and perhaps the community around them hangs in the balance. Here strengths and weaknesses are tested.

Falling Action

During the falling action the conflict unravels. Here the protagonist either wins or loses against the antagonist [enemy, foe]. There may be one final moment of suspense here, in which the final outcome is in doubt.

Dénouement; resolution, revelation, or catastrophe

Here conflicts are resolved, questions are answered, intentions made clear and a balance for individual and society is created. Cathartic release can happen here. There can be either a positive or negative ending.

CHAPTER TWO
IDEAS IN GENERAL

The A-Ha Moment
What to Write
Borrowing from Great Writers
Oops Factor – Similarities or Plagiarism
Writer's Block vs The Fountain of Imagination
True Writer's Block

> *Let's get one thing clear right now, shall we. There is no Idea Dump, no Story Central, no Island of the Buried Bestsellers; good story ideas seem to come quite literally from nowhere, sailing at you right out of an empty sky: two previously unrelated ideas come together and make something new under the sun. Your job isn't to find these ideas but to recognize them when they show up.*
>
> *Stephen King "On Writing"*

THE A-HA MOMENT

Take a moment to not think

How does spontaneity and creativity work? Paul McCartney said that songs are just in the air. That makes sense, for it is where the word inspiration comes from. To inspire has more than one meaning. To take in breath, to inhale is one and the other is to pass ideas to others- ideas that move us. Surely that is what we do as storytellers? These stories are waiting in the ether for us to discover them. Phil Beadle in his wonderful book on creativity 'Dancing about Architecture' cites the writing of James Webb from his book 'A Technique for Producing Ideas'.

It runs like this:
Step One – Gather your raw material
Step Two – Digest the Material
Step Three – DON'T THINK
Step Four – Wait for the 'A-ha Moment' to arrive and be prepared for it.
Step Five – Expose your idea to the light of day and see if it stands up to the glare. Is it strong enough to stand analysis and critiquing?

It is steps three and four that are the essence of what happens in creativity but all five stages are equally important.

'Writer' suggests all kinds of places to gather your raw material such as watching and listening to real life, recommended reading and viewing. It also gives you ways of understanding and digesting the material you have gathered.

Step Three **Don't Think** is the moment when you have given up consciously thinking about your subject. If that doesn't make sense, ask yourself this. Have you ever given up on solving a perplexing problem after hours of struggle, only to have the answer come to you in a blinding flash? 'Of course, that's it! Why didn't I see that before?'

Being fully prepared is necessary for the truly great moments of inspiration.

Then comes the intangible; that special something in the air!

And finally, you look at the idea from every angle and say is this the one? Is this what I have been searching for? Is this the story that will hold my attention and the readers for hundreds of hours?

The **'A-ha Moment'** is truly a gift from on high! Thanks Zeus, Odin, the Goddess, existence or the woman on the late night train, whomever......thank you!

WHAT TO WRITE

What shall I write?

What have I read that I really like?

Do I want to follow in the footsteps and style of my favourite writer?

Is it a good idea to follow in those footsteps?

Will my work just be a lukewarm copy or will it offer something new and engaging?

Worse still, what if I have no ideas worth writing about?

All valid questions and ones that each of us have asked at times.

DRAWING FROM REAL LIFE

Believe in what you experience for it is valid source material

Novice writers often look at the elaborate characters, settings and powerfully engrossing plots that established writers have created and are over-awed if not intimidated. How did they do that?

Firstly, those writers have drawn from their own lives. What they have observed in others and what they have found within themselves is finetuned into characters and situations within their novels. When you think about it, **this is your primary source material** – what you observe in the world around you, for it is what you know best. Whether the story is contemporary or set in some time in the past, whether it is fantasy or realist is secondary to finding a truth in the writing.

As writers, we observe and draw on what happens in the real world and by that, I mean more than just incident. The truth is that human needs and longings have not changed. Your character might be a Roman Centurion or a peasant woman selling potpourri but their desires and how they strive to attain what they want has not changed since we learnt to walk upright and use language.

Coupled with our acute observations of human nature goes careful planning and detailed research and finally writing flair. Step by step we will look at how to create this quartet – Drawing from Real Life/Complete Story Structure/Research and creating your own poetic style.

BORROWING FROM GREAT WRITERS

A brief look at universal ideas, themes and how they have been used by numerous writers

Do I want to follow in the footsteps and style of my favourite writer? Is it a good idea to follow in those footsteps? Will my work just be a lukewarm copy or will it offer something new and engaging?

When I was a boy I thought that my favourite band *'The Beatles'* were extraordinarily original. I still do. But at the time, I didn't realize how much they were borrowing from their mentors and peers. Like all clever creators they took from around themselves and what came before and then made it their own.

THEY BORROWED AND REMODELLED AND UPDATED THEIR INFLUENCES.

Now let's look at one of the great borrowers of the literary world- Joanne Kathleen Rowling.

In my opinion, the *'Harry Potter'* series is a world of unparalleled brilliance – it is touching, funny, thrilling, terrifying, amazing, beguiling, oddball and intriguing in equal measure. Of course, like crime and science fiction before it, fantasy fiction is not always considered important or great art. But in time her work will sit, with Lewis Carroll and Kenneth Grahame, among the true immortals.

However, Joanne did not write this in a vacuum. She knew to borrow from those who went before and she knew their work thoroughly. Wonderful character names, like Severus Snape or Bathilda Bagshot, use the same sound/ character relationships as both Shakespeare and Dickens utilized. {See **CHARACTER NAMES Chapter Four**}

Her writing has echoes of Enid Blyton and Thomas Hughes' *'Tom Brown's Schooldays'*, the Grimm Brothers, Charles Perrault, Tolkien and the Bible plus references to 20th century history.

She knew that to create a resonant and engaging epic she would have to write something that touches our deepest fears and our desire for love, recognition and family.

She would reveal prejudices, the horrors of racism and the power of noble sacrifice. By drawing on the history of Nazi Germany and the Gethsemane and Calvary story she creates a world that begins like a Famous Five adventure but ends as a towering saga - a study of bigotry, despotism, the power of love and a willingness to die for others.

The point here is that a good writer is one who knows their craft. They know the nuts and bolts of story creation; they know how to build a story using all the fundamentals of storytelling.

But just as importantly they understand what other writers have done. They absorb and borrow from them. And because they love and study literature they will naturally absorb stories from all cultures and eras and these will become part of their background knowledge. Then they work at these ideas and make not a copy but something new- the children of the characters and ideas that came before.

So, don't copy slavishly, borrow wilfully and make it your own creatively.

THE OOPS FACTOR – SIMILARITIES OR PLAGIARISM

Something tells me I've heard that before

We have so many stories within us, not only the ones we are creating but also the ones we have absorbed from all sorts of sources, in our lifetime. Sometimes you will find yourself creating a story, believing that it is all your own. It comes to your attention that it is similar to someone else's story. This cannot be helped. Some writers will discard it! Others will file it for use, as the springboard for something else they will write and then rework it to the point where it is only vaguely similar.

If you kept a story in your head it was probably because it was a good one, even if it was not yours. You are on the right track and it shows that you recognize qualities in stories that are worth investigating.

New stories will come to you and some of them will have something from the past - something that you may have kept unconsciously. You may choose to discard or you may choose to rework it.

Each writer has their own approach to this dilemma. Some will not go near a story that is too close to an established one and others will toy with it and sometimes pull it apart and reconstruct it. If you go down this road you must be careful. It simply cannot be so close to the original story that you could be accused of **PLAGIARISING.**

WRITER'S BLOCK VS THE FOUNTAIN OF IMAGINATION

Self-criticism is not the same as quality control. Getting out of your own way to allow a creative flow

Many writers complain that their ideas dry up. They feel they suffer from writer's block. This can happen for any number of reasons but we need to find ways to get out of this and there are processes that this book offers to help you when you become stuck.

Does the kind of block you are having look something like this?

"I cannot move forward because I don't believe in my ideas. Everything I come up with is rubbish!"

We all want to exercise quality control over what we make but be careful that you are not slipping into the mind game of 'What about? …. no that won't do!'

UNDERSTAND THE DIFFERENCE BETWEEN EXERCISING QUALITY CONTROL AND BEING UNDERMINED BY YOURSELF.

GET OUT OF THIS HEADSPACE IMMEDIATELY IF YOU ARE IN IT, YOU ARE BEING JUDGEMENTAL.

All ideas are small when they first come along; the trick is to let them be. They will change and grow, if you allow them.

Do not compare your little idea with the scope and depth of finished works. *'Harry Potter'* began as an idea about a boy, who discovers he is a wizard and goes off to Wizarding School. This is a small idea but the more the idea is played with, the more concepts fall into place. Sometimes they come so thick and fast that it seems that you are getting the whole story in one go but really the ideas come one after another.

In fact, for J.K. Rowling the ideas came so fast that within four hours she had most of the plotline worked out. But it is also true that many hours, days, weeks, months, years of preparation had gone before. All the writing and reading you do is preparation for the stories you will write later.

But how do you get from an initial idea to a finished storyline and a self-contained world in fiction?

Many of Rowling's ideas were inspired by the books she had read in childhood, at school, in early adulthood and at university. Here she was preparing and gathering raw material. Let's look at some of the ideas and their antecedents.

Who does Harry live with? He lives with a family who treat him badly [This is the *Cinderella* Story reworked].

His parents have died – he is an orphan. This idea was used numerous times, in the previous decades by Roald Dahl [James in *'James and the Giant Peach'* and Boy in *'The Witches'*], prior to J.K. Rowling utilising it. Dickens uses the orphan motif in *'Great Expectations'* and *'Oliver Twist'*, as many other writers have done, down through the ages. {See **The Power of the Orphan. Chapter Six**} Rowling admits to having spent a great deal of time in her young adult life reading Dickens and Tolkien and these influences are apparent in her books. Both Rowling and Tolkien use the character name of *'The Dark Lord'* for a start.

If we have an orphan then we have the promise of a journey, both emotionally and physically, to find love and a new family.

How did the hero's parents die? If they were killed then we could have themes to do with that evil coming after him. This in turn pushes him toward avenging the crime, of defeating the evil that led to their deaths- of facing his nemesis.

So **FROM A SIMPLE IDEA**

Schoolboy with supernatural powers
ADD
Bitter experiences in family life
ADD
Dead Parents
ADD
Knowing that he is in danger still/ avenging their deaths.
ADD
Facing his nemesis.

So, you can see that as simple ideas become elaborated, we are dealing with much larger issues – family, good versus evil, facing fears and so on. Now a simple idea is starting to sound sophisticated, possibly even profound.

Let's look at this process again, starting with a small idea. The terms in brackets describe components of story building that we have not covered yet. Some terms relate to story building found in Writer I and some are specific to The Hero's Journey which can be found in Writer II.

Try and take them in and return later to this passage and see how many more you understand.

One evening at a fairground, a young girl buys a ticket for a carousel.

[INITIAL SET UP]

ADD

But something happens on that merry go round- she sees something out of the corner of her eye. She is not sure of what she has seen in the reflecting mirrors, as she rides the prancing pony.

[FIRST GLIMPSE OF OTHER WORLD]

ADD

At home that night, she is disturbed by what she has seen and conveys it to her sister.

[ESTABLISHING HOME SETTING]

Her house is poor, in fact the rent is overdue and they have been given an eviction notice.

[FIRST COMPLICATION]

ADD

The next evening, she returns to the fairground. The ticket seller tells her that they have been expecting her.

[HIGHER POWERS WATCHING/THRESHOLD GUARDIAN]

ADD

She rides the horse but after two rotations she jumps off and approaches the counter clockwise rotating centre. There she sees herself in the mirror, in another world.

[DEEPER INTO THE MYSTERY]

ADD

At school, the following day she relates the tale to her best friend. That morning she is chosen to represent the school in competition. She runs home, that afternoon, to tell her parents of this exciting turn of events.

[ESTABLISHING COMPANION/PROMISE OF GLORY]

ADD

She arrives to find her father has hired a moving van. They will be packing over the next two days and she will need to move to a new school.

[THE TICKING CLOCK]

ADD

She goes back that night but there is only a vacant lot where the carnival once stood.

[SECOND COMPLICATION/QUEST BEGINS]

WE WILL STOP HERE.

You can see that from one simple idea – '*A young girl buys a ticket for a carousel*'- we have moved into something involving mystery, loss, dislocation, family upheaval, potential to succeed or fail and the promise of glory. This is no longer a small idea; larger themes are developing here.

Where did all these ideas come from? They just simply linked to one another- they came from the Fountain of the Imagination.

A writer's mind should always be making associations, seeing ideas that can hang together to create a story.

TRUE WRITER'S BLOCK

Writer's Block can be where your ideas literally dry up. This can last for hours, days or weeks. All you can do is be patient. Use some of the templates and story starters suggested throughout the book and simply play with the possibilities. Do not judge, just allow the ideas to come, no matter how strange. Sleep on it and look at the storylines again in the morning. Often a way out comes with relaxation and time.

Writer's Block also occurs when you have definitive characters and a developed situation within a storyline and have boxed yourself into a corner, with your protagonists and the plot. Your ideas for the next stage of the story do not fit with how the characters would behave or how the story arc is developing. You just can't make it ring true.

All you can do is wait for inspiration and insight to arrive. Keep writing even if it has nothing to do with your main story and this will often serve to free things up. Solving Plot and Character problems will become clearer later when we deal with character and story arc.

CHAPTER THREE
FINDING IDEAS FOR YOUR STORY

Free Writing
Exercise 2
Word/Idea Associations
Exercise 3
Single Incident What Ifs
Exercise 4
Random What Ifs
Exercise 5
Exercise 6
Sequential What Ifs
What Ifs that Play against Type, logic and Expectation
Exercise 7
Story Templates
Exercise 8
Like a Gorilla in a Wetsuit/like a Chainsaw in a Cradle/Salmon Ambulance
Exercise 9

Brainstorming and Spitballing

Let me say this maxim one more time. A writer's mind should always be making associations, seeing things that can hang together to make a story.

But you are not just looking for plot and incident you are also looking for character and conflict. If you come up with a story idea immediately ask yourself what is the emotional undercurrent – not just what happens but what is desired and what is at stake. [See Conflict Chapter Six]

FREE WRITING

If you have no idea what to write initially, it often helps to just put pen to paper or fingers to keyboard.

EXERCISE 2.

Begin with words- Man, woman, child, once in a distant land, the sky darkened as, she stepped from the train as, the man waited in the shadows till….. Don't judge, just watch things. Your mind will start to put pieces together.

Here is another way to help it along.

WORD/IDEA ASSOCIATION

Create a lucky dip of words/ideas that can be pulled out and associated together, to form story suggestions. Fill in ideas, possibilities under these headings -

Characters   Quests
Locations   Desires

Jeopardies/Dangers   Names
Misfortunes   Companions
                     Skills
                     Random Thoughts

EXERCISE 3.

Now liberally dip into these. They can exist in folders in your computer or as cards in individual boxes in your study. Sit them side by side as lists and free associate one idea from the first list with a dozen or more possibilities from the second list. Then take these two ideas, with twenty possibilities from a third list and so on.

Let the ideas freely associate together and allow time to just look at them. Sometimes the most surprising combinations occur through this kind of arrangement.

Here is one possibility that might have come out - A one legged man/Tropical resort/contagious disease/ his boat's engine fails/he has a map/his boat's skipper is called Rex/Telepathy.

Other times you will look at the groupings and start to rearrange them because they are less than satisfactory. You add something and eliminate something else.

Either way, processes are in motion that will lead to story creation.

An Example of WORD/IDEA ASSOCIATION LISTS

Characters	Locations	Jeopardies/ Dangers	Misfortunes
Orphan Child	Tropics	Unable to swim	Shipwreck
Cruel Gaoler	19th C. London	Illiterate	Tuberculosis
Unemployed	Scotland	Hears voices	Arrested

Farmhand

Quests	Desires	Names	Companions
Seeking	Love	Camille	Mikey
Recognition	family	Caleb	Alphonse
Kidnapped child	Fortune	Johnnie	Pascal

Skills	Random Thoughts
Ability with rope	Whistles constantly
Fluent in 3 languages	Missing the middle finger
Great mathematical skill	A joke for every occasion

WHAT IFS {SINGLE INCIDENT}

AUTHORS CONSTANTLY THINK OF STORY POSSIBILITIES

To maintain that skill, we need to keep in practise. 'What Ifs' are a game and an exercise that you should do on a regular basis?

You create as many possibilities and variations on an initial idea as you can. You are not required to turn them into full stories but as a way of exercising your creative mind it is second to none.

Look at an example.

It is dark. The moon has gone down a half hour ago and the highway stretches out into the black inkiness. The headlights draw the ghosts of trees out of the dark and then they are gone. In the distance one single red eye glows –growing larger, a deeper crimson.

A turn of the corner and the red eye is revealed. A car burns by the roadside; a small man is crumpled on the verge with his head slumped forward.

A woman stands screaming, her fists held above her head, her mouth wide, frozen open.

And then they disappear behind back into the night.

- Let us look at this scenario and create explanations – 'What Ifs' to explain this incident.
- The engine has caught fire and a family's lives have reached financial ruin. This car is all they own. He is defeated and she is distressed.
- The man slumped forward is injured. His assailant has disappeared into the darkness. He has set fire to the car so that the man and the woman cannot follow.
- In a war-torn country, a car has rolled over an incendiary mine in the road. With no car, the escapees have no way of escape. The explosion and the flames will soon bring the enemy. All is lost.

EXERCISE 4.

Someone is trapped inside ……….. {Finish this. Find your own explanation for the man and the woman} There is any number of explanations. Think of a five more of your own.

RANDOM WHAT IFS

Here is another kind of 'What If'. Instead of being based on a single incident, these are various random possibilities.

What if dogs reverted to wild instincts and lost their need to have human companions?

What if you stopped machines every time you came near them?

What if you kept waking to find objects in your room you did not recognise? That weren't there the night before?

What if a voice in your head told you of events still to happen and what choice to make, which led to further and greater successes? Then one day one of these choices leads to a tragedy! [D. H. Lawrence wrote a short story based on this premise]

EXERCISE 5.

Think of other story starters? Think of at least five every day? Create a folder to keep them in.

Later they may be used to start a story or create a complication. Or perhaps they will inspire another story based on your original idea, but different. Note, all ideas are acceptable here. No idea is too outrageous or ridiculous. Just write them down and who knows where they will lead?

Here is one more example of a single incident 'What If'

A girl of seventeen stands on a street corner, under a streetlight. The road stretches off into the neon lit city. In the distance, the red tail lights of a vehicle disappear over the hill.

What are some of the reasons she might be there?

- She has left home for good and is about to disappear to the big city to escape her family and her suffocating life.
- She has been transported here from another time. She has arrived here to alter the future. [Well-worn but still usable]
- She has lost her memory and does not know who or where she is. In a few moments, someone will deceive her into believing that she is their daughter. [A preposterous idea but the challenge is to make it work.]

EXERCISE 6.

Suggest some more explanations for this scene? Create five more?

SEQUENTIAL WHAT IFS [WITHIN ONE STORY]

This is what an author does constantly within a short story, a novella or novel. You ask yourself what if this happens and then what if that happens in reply but all of it is directly connected to the development of the plot. It might look something like this.

- What if our main character Carla arrives in the town where her father Rick has been secretly living for the last twenty-two years?
- What if she gets a job in the office of the timber mill where he works as a driver?
- What if because he has changed his name and they have not seen each other since she was a child, she does not recognize him?
- What if he watches her from a distance trying to keep her safe but she has had almost no parental guidance and she is 'off the rails'.
- What if she becomes involved with a local high-risk taker called Keenan?
- What if Keenan is planning a robbery?
- What if Keenan offers to take on Rick as his right-hand man in the crime.
- What if Carla is excited by the prospect of becoming an outlaw and wants to become part of their plans.

- What if the reason Rick is living secretly in this town is that he doesn't want his past to catch up with him, as it will cost him his freedom. But, in order to save Carla, he is going to have to make himself known to the authorities.

The story above has been created as a series of interconnected events/incidents but notice that as the story develops the stakes rise. We move from plot and character to emotional core/conflict. To save his child he must put his own freedom at risk.

For further examples of this kind of story creation see the 'What Ifs' that Charles Dickens appears to have applied to *'A Tale of Two Cities'* in the **IRONY** section.

'WHAT IFS' WHICH PLAY AGAINST TYPE, LOGIC OR EXPECTATION

Stephen King in his insightful book *'On Writing'* talks of creating a character and storyline that plays against the perceived view that assassins are misguided and antisocial for his novel *"The Dead Zone'*.

He invents an assassin who intends to kill a particularly insidious politician, one we have grown to despise and whose actions threaten life on earth. This is a wonderful example of reverse thinking; of creating a story that flies in the face of conventional wisdom.

In Robert Harris's book *'Fatherland'* the Berlin police are investigating a murder in a united Europe, several decades after the Second World War. Hitler has won and Germany rules a vast empire, in relative peace and prosperity. The story is set around the seventy fifth birthday celebrations of the Fuehrer – a leader who has presided over a united Europe, in a climate of abundance and security since 1945. Hitler is a somewhat benevolent father figure and the horrors of the 'Holocaust' are unknown.

EXERCISE 7.

Think of five 'What Ifs' as potential plots, that are the opposite of the way society is today or how popular consensus sees the world?

STORY TEMPLATES

Here is a story starter given to me in a writer's workshop by the brilliant writer James Roy, author of *'Town'*.

You just fill in the gaps and immediately a story begins to take shape.

ONCE........

EVERYDAY.......

UNTIL ONE DAY......

BECAUSE OF THAT.......

BECAUSE OF THAT........

UNTIL FINALLY.....

These temporal links are not just incident. 'Because of that' is where the plot develops but it also puts the protagonist in an emotional position, where they must make choices. 'Because of that' the main character is terrified, incensed, heartbroken, maligned - dozens of emotional potentialities that interact with others.

EXERCISE 8.

Take this template and create a story. Taken on its own it will allow you to create a short story.

From there you can mix it up with 'What Ifs' and 'Backstory' and larger stories will form. Keep adding to it from source material and from further techniques we will explore and you will begin to see a novella or a novel forming

Here is another story starter that you might use to get you thinking about your characters and what kind of journey they are going on, especially emotionally.

LOVE/FEAR Ask yourself what is it that your focal character most loves and what they most fear?

WANT/NEED Ask what that character most wants or desires but also what they most need. Often while they know what they want, they are unaware of what they need. Often what they need is going to be provided for them, through trial and tribulation, in the form of a life lesson- something that will help them grow and come to a larger realization.

LIKE A GORILLA IN A WETSUIT/LIKE A CHAINSAW IN A CRADLE

There is a line in a Bob Dylan song that runs *'Jewels and binoculars hang from the head of the mule'**. This has always grabbed me; I don't need to know what it means, if it means anything at all. It's like an image from a dream. It works because these are words/ideas that sit together that wouldn't ordinarily be there – jewels, binoculars and mule.

This leads to the idea that all original writers grasp – putting things together, that aren't usually associated peaks your readers' imagination and hopefully initially causes all kinds of creative synapses to start sparking in you. So many possibilities are revealed by placing unlikely things together.

Start by having a look at the title of this section - 'Like a Gorilla in a Wetsuit'. It is obviously humorous but are there other possibilities? Could this be an animal story? What about Science Fiction?

What about 'Like a Chainsaw in a Cradle'? How does this make you feel? Does this one have a more sinister aspect?

These questions bring us to our next stage called...

SALMON AMBULANCE

This is a very surreal technique but its purpose is to put the most unlikely things together, as story stimuli. Like 'Word/Idea Association', it can consist of lists. Except that these are lists of objects that are as varied and random as possible.

For example, what would a cross between an ambulance and a salmon look like? How would something like this come about? Try to picture it in your minds' eye. Come to think of it, what is a minds' eye, isn't that two things that don't go together but we somehow know what they mean? This is an image created by Shakespeare, who was the master of placing incongruent words and images together to create new forms.

Try to picture a salmon ambulance. Put together other

---

* *'Visions of Johanna'* by Bob Dylan - *Blonde on Blonde* Album combinations. What kinds of surreal images and ideas do you create?

The more you do this, the more the juxtaposition of odd assortments of things will fit. You may find you eventually don't need to refer to lists. Perhaps you do this so naturally that you don't need lists from the start.

Here is what a list might look like -

Gumboot	stethoscope	overcoat	stool
Cannon	windmill	wingnut	moustache
Cooking pot	easel	umbrella	porcupine
Chocolate	bicycle	bellows	claw hammer
Serpent	chess board	butter churn	eyeball
Clarinet	eyeball	lizard	axe

You can keep building on these as you come across a word that describes something unusual like 'monocle' or 'amethyst' or 'salamander'.

Add to these some very common words such as shoe, window and chair.

Putting the most common with the more unusual makes the combination even stranger and more evocative. For example – leather spoon, thunder vinegar, a staircase of water or eyebrows made of cement.

EXERCISE 9.

Take the sample table from above and create ten fantastical and bizarre combinations. See if they conjure up stories to validate their existence. Where will this lead? I can't tell. However, imagination is as huge as the ocean – its possibilities are endless. Jump in and swim and who knows on what shore you will wash up.

BRAINSTORMING.....

Writing pads, Whiteboards, Mind Maps and large sheets of plain paper

Brainstorming often works using a template like a 'Mind Map' {find one in **Chapter Seven**} but can also work by simply putting down all the ideas that come to you, on a writing pad/exercise book/large sheet of paper. Brainstorming can be a solitary act or a group activity. Brainstorming may take days or weeks, as the ideas expand and connect with other ideas. Sometimes brainstorming may happen in a matter of minutes or hours.

....AND SPITBALLING

Gathering with like-minded writers to find a new slant on character and plot

'Spitballing' is a term that belongs to American screenwriters but it can just as easily apply to novelists and writers in general. It comes from baseball and is a term for an illegal pitch of the ball. So, in writing terms, we are talking about an unexpected, unorthodox pitch of an idea. The similar phrase 'an idea from leftfield' is another baseball term.

'Spitballing' is a gathering of writers, who all focus in on one person's work and approach it from their own points of view. Because the other writers have no preconceived ideas about the plot or characters they can suggest all kinds of ways of approaching the material that the original writer did not think of. They are not locked in or have attachments to characters. What they suggest at times can be shocking to the author. 'What if the main character was the opposite sex?' or 'What if the situation becomes more dangerous because the other character is mentally unstable?' These kinds of left field suggestions can completely throw a writer at the time but if they are taken away and thought about then new ideas and possibilities arrive. Spitballing is done with other members of the profession - people who know what they are talking about and can help reshape your work. This can be extraordinarily helpful, especially if you are in the grip of writer's block.

*Finding other members of the profession for advice and support {and legal protection} is why we all join Writers Guilds and Societies of Authors. Do a search for them in your state or country – they are invaluable for helping you on the road to becoming a successful writer,

We have looked at the three-act structure and ways to get ideas as story starters, suppose now that you now have a story idea and a basic plot, where to next?

CHAPTER FOUR
PEOPLING YOUR STORY

Building Characters
Backstory
Exercise 10
Character Motivation
Character Names
Exercise 11
Exercise 12
Place names {and some more characters}
Writing Dialogue
Finding your Voices
Differentiating Principal Characters

BUILDING CHARACTERS

Having empathy with your characters, even the vile ones

We identify with characters because we begin to live their fictional lives, experience their thoughts, embrace their desires and feel their fears and indecisions. And of course, we see them in action.

This is an obvious thing to say but let's look at this from the viewpoint of being the author of these characters. As the creator, it is an absolute necessity to know your characters inside out, to have empathy with them, even the vilest of them.

Writers often talk about their characters having a life of their own and dictating the direction a story will take. What they mean is that a character takes on a defined personality and their actions push a developing story in a certain direction. Sometimes this is not how the author would have originally planned it. It becomes **'No I can't do this way; my character wouldn't do that. That is out of character!'**

Your characters need to be fleshed out; to behave in ways that make sense, that resonate with who they are. Characters should be real enough to be consistent and yet at times be surprising.

This can only happen by creating a life for your characters- using a process called a BACKSTORY

BACKSTORY

Worldly and Personal Attributes

Backstory is the 'behind the scenes' life story of your character; of all the hurts, loves, disillusionments, aspirations that went before our narrative begins.

Some writers need to get this basic planning down first before embarking on their story.

For others, too much planning gets in the way of creativity and so they come to this a little later. It is often where they will go after they have created their characters and their story as a story plan or as a first draft and now want to flesh them out. At this point they want to make the characters more real for themselves. It is important to note that some or none of this may appear in the finished story. It is there for the writer and is designed to help them have a better understanding of character, plot and motivation. It can also solve plot problems and free up a case of Writer's Block.

Fleshing them out can be about appearance, size, social standing, confidence or lack of, race and nationality and most importantly motivation. It is also based on class, religion, upbringing, family and other factors you will find in the BACKSTORY PROFILE {below}.

WORLDLY ATTRIBUTES
Kind of Family
Class
Position in family
Confidence out in the world
Religion
Political attitudes/associations
Social standing
Occupation
Successes
Failures
Catastrophe Natural
Catastrophe Man made

PERSONAL ATTRIBUTES
Gender
Age
Race
Size
Shape
Physical positives
Physical negatives
Hair colour
Eye colour
Skin colour
Voice tone
Physical ticks
Physical features
Psychological state
Obsessions/Wishes/Fears

This is not a complete list but it does start you thinking about all the social and personal aspects that make up a character.

You will come up with more attributes than what is here. Keep a file for Backstory.

Think about your own life and how the events in your life have shaped you. Think about how you appear to others and how that affects you. Think about how you see yourself and whether that has an influence on your success in the world.

Here are other considerations that relate to a character profile.

Where was your character born?

Are they carrying a deep secret?

Have they been in love and do they have a broken heart?

Who are the people that surround and support your character? They reveal much about your main character.

Does your character have an attachment to a place, object or memory that reveals something important about them?

As you read stories look at how the author has created characters and make notes. Build up a spreadsheet of characteristics you can utilize.

Let us create a character for a story. This person is a twisted, unhappy person who wants to punish the world for all that has happened to him. In a story we might create, he will be an antagonist and the source of much of the complications. Not necessarily a villain but someone who makes life difficult for others. Perhaps a protagonist with a long emotional journey ahead of them.

Note - Often creating a backstory will suggest the way your story will go or alter the direction of a pre-existing storyline. Sometimes it can be the catalyst for creating a story in the first place. It becomes a kind of EXPANDED WHAT IF.

CHARACTER NAME-Fingal Swain

Gender - Male

Age- 40 although he could be older as his face is twisted and wrinkled.

Race - White /Caucasian

Size- Small / 5 Foot 3 inches/ 160 cm

Shape- a man with almost no neck

Physical positives- a fine dress sense

Physical negatives- Not a pleasant man to look at but no scars or deformities apart from left hand.

Hair colour- Brown with greying tips

Hair style – long at the back/ short at the sides/balding on top

Eye colour- pale blue eyes

Skin colour – pale from staying inside

Voice tone – a deep and hypnotic tone

Physical ticks – a tendency to look sideways with suspicion

Physical features – a scar across his left hand

Family relationship- A family in which little love was shown and the way to win respect was to outdo your siblings

*Class-*Upper middle class

Position in family- middle child/one younger sister and he remain

Confidence out in the world- manipulates the situation /confident in his abilities to control others

Religion- Not applicable

Political attitudes/associations - apolitical

Social standing- Respected member of society/he hides behind this

Occupation- Owner of a number of clothes factories

Successes- Inherited his parents' money when his older brother and parents died.

Failures- Bullied at school/ not liked/ no relationships

Catastrophe [Natural] – Not applicable.

Catastrophe [Man made] only survivor of car crash where he gained a scar on his left hand. Sister was not in car at time.

Picture this person?

Is there enough information for you to form in your head the kind of character Fingal Swain is? Can you begin to see how he would behave based on his background?

Not all backstories need to be this elaborate. If you were writing a short story the background of a main character would not be so detailed. This is the backstory of a character from a novella or a novel or for the script of a feature film. An elaborate backstory is necessary for you to understand character and story arc but a writer only uses as much as is needed in the story and no more. Characters are almost always thumbnail sketches that allow the readership to fill in the gaps and create their own mental picture of the characters.

Here is a short story I created several years after creating this profile. I did however set this story earlier than my forty-year old in the backstory. Other facts and characteristics remain unchanged.

Fingal Swain sat in his oak panelled office behind a large mahogany desk. Above him was a stark oil painting of his father, the founder of Swains, the largest textile mill and the major employer in the county. On his desk was the only photo Fingal had of his whole family together before the car accident – Fingal, his brother Feargal, his younger sister Clara and their domineering father standing behind them, his hand resting proprietorially on the older brother's shoulder. Their mother standing to one side diminished and apprehensive.

It had not been an easy life. Always bettered by Feargal and scorned by his father, he had taken that tenuous sense of self-worth to boarding school, where lonely, abandoned and persecuted he tried to keep to himself.

On his holidays, he would walk the hills and the coastline content to be far away from the family home. There he would draw on the novels and poems that had been his comfort at school. Imprisoned Counts and wronged adventurers, Jacobite warriors, tales of banshees and the little people made the hours disappear, until it was time to find his way home. For Fingal this was all the love he would know; that which he gave to himself.

It was there that he had run across Seamus Pinkerton and his gang of local bovver boys and they took to him in much the same way that birds round on one of their kind that is injured. Bloodied and bruised he had stumbled to the edge of town where he washed his face at the town well. His father would have only use it against him if he was to arrive home dishevelled and having suffered an obvious beating.

Fingal inherited the mill when only he and his sister Clara survived after the crash. And though he had never wanted it, as the director of the company he had the power to decide where cuts would be made on his factory floor. For a moment, he sat there enjoying the exquisite pleasure of what he was about to do. Picking up the phone he said each name slowly and deliberately.

'Pinkerton..........O'Riordan..........Kelly..........McManus, send them in.'

They entered in single file, shoulders stooped, cloth cap in hand and then Pinkerton straightened up and looked Swain in the eyes.

'Ok, we all know why we're here, so don't muck us around. Get it over with.'

But Fingal wasn't going to be rushed. He arched his fingers on the desk as he had seen his father do so many times in his youth. He contemplated them a few moments.

'Well boys, you probably know there's been a downturn in the market. Nothing to be done about that. And so, we have to lay off some people.' He paused for a moment for it to take effect. 'And I'm sorry to say it's you boys.' He said boys twice in a way that made it clear that this had a great deal to do with their youth.

'You ain't sorry in the slightest' said Kelly realizing that humbleness was not going to save his job.

Fingal opened a portfolio on his desk and scanned it, determined to make it clear that he didn't need to converse with them anymore. 'Pick up your wages from the pay office as you go.', he said without looking up. ''And leave your work clothes here or we'll have to charge you for them.'

'You have to give us notice.'

'Yeah, two weeks!' said McManus encouraged by the others.

He looked up after a long pause. 'No, I don't. If you look at your contracts you will see that. Unions days are long gone.'

Pinkerton began to grind one hand into the other. Once more he was the leader of the gang. 'Don't be walkin' the hills anytime soon Swainy .'

'Or drinkin' in The Arms.'

'Oh, you can rest assured I won't be Seamus. You would be the last people on earth I would want to be sharin' a droink wid,' he said imitating a broad country brogue.

For a few moments more they stood there, each thinking about the consequences if they leapt across the desk and took him by the throat. Then as one they turned to go.

It was Pinkerton who turned back from the door. 'A bigger man would forget the things kids do. But I guess you're not a bigger man, are you Swainy?'

Fingal Swain looked up at Pinkerton with a broad, condescending smile.

'No....I guess I'm not.'

He sat in the cavernous room and looked out of the bay window, across the factory yard to the hills beyond. He thought to himself that it felt wrong, that he would have gained a greater feeling of satisfaction but the experience now felt hollow. He watched the four men walk through the factory gates for the last time. The afternoon sun was glinting off the peaks of the hills and somewhere a boy was walking the coast road making up stories.

In this story, the character came first and the story later. But for me it is plot that usually comes first. There are no hard rules on this.

EXERCISE 10

Take the backstory profile and create a character. Perhaps a larger story will arise.

CHARACTER MOTIVATION

Put down that axe Eugene! Why are you acting like a madman? How backstory helps us to understand why our characters behave as they do

Backstory is a great way to understand your characters and at times it will suggest the direction your story will take. Backstory supplies the character's motivation- why they behave in an individual way. As writers, we understand the character's agenda. Readers may not understand that character's motivation at first. Perhaps it will be revealed as the story progresses. But for writers it is essential that we understand a character's motivation, whether it is revealed immediately or later or not at all. The character does things or works positively or negatively towards achieving things because of their background- the life experiences that went before.

It can also supply scenes for your story that flesh out the character and explain to the audience why they do what they do. Some of the backstory can and does appear in a longer piece but perhaps not all of it needs to be in your story. IT IS THERE FOR YOUR UNDERSTANDING AFTER ALL.

And then there are lots of times in life where people behave in ways that are completely unfathomable to us. Sometimes your characters can be like that too. Just don't be too extreme unless that is the kind of character they have become in the story. Even then you must understand why they do what they do.

CHARACTER NAMES

Looking at why and what we name our characters. And what a name can create in the mind of a reader

Some names have a subtle power and are very deliberate in what they set out to do. Tolkien introduces a character into the early stages of the *'The Fellowship of the Ring'* who travels the land. Dark and mysterious, he has a powerful almost threatening demeanour. He is 'a ranger' travelling under the alias 'Strider'- in other words a man who walks boldly and resolutely across the land; a kind of warrior gypsy. Later we will know him as the troubled and reluctant future king Aragorn. But at the beginning, for the sake of the story and the fellowship's need of secrecy, 'Strider' is a perfect **name to create.**

Now imagine you need to create a character that is overbearing and egotistical and brags constantly to his long-suffering friends. Someone who later will be the butt of a 'magical' practical joke and who is a complete pain in the ……. Yes, what better name to call him than 'Bottom the Weaver' -as Shakespeare did in *'Midsummer Night's Dream'*.

Names conjure feelings and emotions; they make associations in the mind. They are a quick and useful way to convey aspects of personality to the reader.

EXERCISE 11

Have a look at this exercise and try to match the character names to the personalities they suggest and then try your hand at creating some of your own.

DICKENS' CHARACTERS

Which character name goes with each description? Answers at end of task

David Copperfield   An orphan with a secret hidden life
Artful Dodger   A clever street thief
Oliver Twist   A young man destined for wealth

SHAKESPEARE'S CHARACTERS

Match these too

Sir Toby Belch   A misshapen monster
Macbeth   A drunken member of the court
Caliban   A nobleman destined to be King

J.K. ROWLING'S CHARACTERS

Look at these names and try to identify what is being suggested by them

Severus Snape
_____

_____

Cornelius Fudge
_____
Victor Krum
_____

EXERCISE 12

Create some names of your own that are suitable for these character traits

YOUR CHARACTERS

_____ - a dark, brooding troubled soldier.

_____ - a fortunate, amazingly lucky traveller of the road.

_____ - a sad and wistful young girl who hungers for a world away from the drudgery of her life.

_____ - a brave older 'frontier' woman, who is both wise and just and guides others along their journey.

Answers and Observations.

Dickens' Characters

David Copperfield- A young man destined for wealth.

Here the allusion is obvious. Firstly, David is a strong choice, being a king's name from the Old Testament; the author is setting him up with some internal strength and some promise. This promise of better things is somewhat suggested by his last name. This is not Goldfield or even Silverfield but Copperfield so the wealth suggested by the name is not enormous. He is possibly destined for great things but there is no guarantee, as some trials and tribulations will need to be faced along the way.

Artful Dodger - A clever street thief

This is probably the most obvious of all and is particularly accurate as it is a 'nickname', possibly one he bestowed upon himself or has been given to him admiringly by Fagin or the rest of the gang of thieves. To steal and not be caught he will need to dodge and weave through crowds artfully

Oliver Twist - An orphan with a secret hidden life

The name suggests not so much a destiny or future as a past –a past in which a 'twist of fate' has robbed him of his place in society. Twist is the name given to him by the orphanage at his birth- the same orphanage that keeps the identity of his mother hidden, till the end.

Oliver is derived from the earlier Olivier which was a popular name among the Norman ruling class after 1066 in Great Britain.

Shakespeare's Characters

Sir Toby Belch - A drunken member of the court

Here is one of Shakespeare's great comic characters and as the name suggests a man who enjoys a drink. He is a loveable rogue who at times behaves appallingly.

Macbeth - A nobleman destined to be King

A man who begins as a brave and noble warrior but who succumbs to his and his wife's ambition and the duplicity of the witches' prophecies. 'Mac' anchors him in a Scottish locale and gives a strong feel to his name and character. But Beth is a girl's name – is this a suggestion of frailty? Is there a suggestion of discord between the two halves of his name? Even if that is not what is intended, it is still there nonetheless? Macbeth was not chosen by Shakespeare, it is a much older story. The implications within the name still hold, though the author of the name is lost to us.

Caliban - A misshapen monster

He is the one-time ruler now twisted and treacherous servant of the magician/ruler of the island in 'The Tempest'. His name is a reworking of the word 'cannibal'.

J.K. Rowling's Characters

You may have gleaned other truths about these characters but here is what I have observed.

Severus Snape

Here we are almost but not quite working in onomatopoeia- that is words that sound the same as the action or object they describe. Snape is a variant on snake, which is the symbol of the Slytherin house, while 'Slytherin' is a variant on slithering- something a snake would do. Notice also that the name contains the word 'sly'- not to be trusted.

Here also we are dealing with sibilance – the use of words that are hissing in sound - Severus Snape/ Salazar Slytherin/

parseltongue. Severus Snape can be described as silent; often appearing unnoticed behind Harry and friends when they are talking, suspicious as he is always doubtful of Harry's motives, sneering and yet finally revealed as sincere for it is Harry he has chosen to protect.

Cornelius Fudge

Cornelius is an old Roman name but it is Fudge that is the interesting choice here. It might allude to confectionary but it is more likely to imply dishonesty. People who' fudge something' are those that fake something. To fudge is to get away with the appearance of doing what was required or intended only. This is how we see many politicians and Cornelius Fudge is definitely a politician.

Victor Krum

Victor Krum is a name that sends mixed messages to the reader. On the one hand his first name implies one who wins, who is victorious. But his second name, while possibly being able to be said as a strong European surname, carries with it a slightly comic tone.

Crumbs are all that is left over from bread or cake and to act 'crummy' is to behave in a poor or dishonourable way. While he is admired by Ron and even mooned over by Hermione he is not going to be a true hero within the narrative.

Character names are a form of shorthand; a way of telegraphing to the audience who a character is. Michael Connelly called his detective Hieronymus Bosch or Harry

Bosch for short. The reason? Because Harry found himself in a city so corrupt it reminded the author of the painting *'The Garden of Worldly Delights'*, a depiction of torment and corruption by the original Bosch painted in the 1500's. So, Harry Bosch was apt. Of course, you may want to disguise the nature of your character and give them a name that belies their true intentions or their eventual denouement. In Orwell's *'1984'*, Winston Smith is an example of this. Smith is the most common name in the English-speaking world which makes the protagonist an *'everyman'* character. Winston reminds the reader of the determined wartime Prime Minister Churchill who had just led Great Britain out of its' darkest years. So, a name with mixed messages perhaps.

PLACE NAMES [AND SOME MORE CHARACTER NAMES]

From Bleak House to Mordor

Places set a mood and even have a character of their own within a story. Let's look at the sounds of both letters and words to help create place names.

Individual letters of the alphabet work similarly to notes in music- some are bass, some are treble and others fall in between. 'D' and 'B' for instance are Bass while 'E' and 'I' are higher in pitch and therefore Treble.

Do not confuse this with the notes within an octave. We are talking language here and not western scale music. Notice where the sounds form in your mouth and this will indicate where the sounds and words fall within a pitch continuum. As well as pitch, some words have a harsher, more percussive sound e.g. Orcs, Urakai, Gollum. Others have a softer, warmer more flowing sound such as Hobbiton, Barrow Downs, Galadriel and Gandalf.

Let's look deeper at the places and names used in Tolkien's *'Lord of the Rings'* – Mordor, Moria, Mount Doom and Sauron are all sombre, darker sounding words and so fit with the oppressive atmosphere they are trying to create. When you hear the word Mordor what comes to mind? Surely it is the crime of homicide. Sauron conjures up thoughts of its' Greek root 'SAUR' meaning lizard, hardly surprising when we remember that Tolkien was a linguist.

And what do we see in names like Rivendell and Lothlorien? Firstly, they are treble in sound, much lighter, friendly not ominous. A dell is a valley and so there is a suggestion of a 'river flowing through a valley'. It is the site of both the forming of the 'Fellowship of the Nine' but also the uneasy alliance between dwarves and elves. Riven- to divide could also possibly be appropriate.

If we built a living space at the top of a house we call it a loft. We also use the word 'Lofty' to describe 'lofty ambitions and lofty ideals', implying their elevated status. The word 'Lore' means the accumulated beliefs and traditions of a community. Are these ideas implicit in Lothlorien - a place where noble wise elves live in the trees? These are only suggestions but they do illustrate that writers think long and hard about what they name people and places.

WRITING DIALOGUE

Dialogue as information and as emotional subtext

Dialogue should flow, it should be easy to read and it will serve many purposes.

DIALOGUE SERVING STORY

Dialogue, I believe should serve plot. But how elaborate that dialogue is can only be determined by the writer. Do not be fooled into thinking that dialogue needs to be overly revealing. Often the dialogue will imply things that the incidents and reactions will illuminate. Here is an example of dialogue kept to a minimum but still being revealing because of how it is placed in the surrounding text –

1936

Ron dragged himself from his bed and pulled on his clothes and his working boots.

His older brother slept on. He knew better than to wake him but his younger brother however could be roused. Gordon groaned and rolled over, desperate for one or two more moments in the warmth and the dark. But his brother was persistent.

'We've gotta go.'

'Aurgh!'

'Now.'

The cold air snapped at their hands and faces as they stumbled in the half-light to the bakery. There, every morning, they would gather up the horse droppings into paper bags and place them in the billycart they had built from fruit boxes and pram wheels.

And together for two hours they pulled their ship of trade through the backstreets of Belmore, selling manure to local gardeners at sixpence a bag.

If they were lucky, and the bosses weren't watching, the bakers would slip them two or three buns fresh from the oven. They would put them in between their shirt and their singlet to keep them warm. When the bread cooled they would eat it on the way to school, a few shillings richer than at dawn.

This dialogue serves to colour the description and it nuances the characters. But we could have told this scene without any dialogue at all. It is subtle, understated; but as there is only five words it adds to a feel rather than providing information. Nonetheless, there are things that we can glean from even this brief snippet. The speaker is industrious and determined. He has a level of authority that is transmitted in his commands. Language like this may be short and to the point but it also can colour a scene and give it extra depth. It is vital that a writer understands the many uses of dialogue.

EMOTIONAL SUBTEXT DIALOGUE

Dialogue is an indicator of what your character feels. Sometimes this is a direct expression of real passions- 'I love you', 'I hate you'.

Sometimes it says one thing but means another, often the opposite of what is spoken.

'Money means nothing to me.'
'Of course, I intend to stay.'
'Believe me, if I could take your place I would.'
'This hurts me more than it does you.'*

INFORMATION DIALOGUE

Some dialogue is necessary to allow the main characters, and therefore the reader, to gain information that will carry the story along.

The nature of menace or evil

The task at hand and the dangers to be faced.

The doubts that are shared about the odds against succeeding.

Obstacles that need to be surmounted to achieve our goals.

Ideas, suspicions, revelations, observations about other characters.

The needs and desires of a character and their longing to have them recognised and responded to.

INFORMATION DIALOGUE CAN BE TOP HEAVY WITH FACTS AND NOT SOUND LIKE TRUE CONVERSATION. THIS KIND OF DIALOGUE OFTEN SOUNDS CLUNKY AND IS CALLED 'EXPOSITION'. TRY TO AVOID THIS KIND OF WRITING. {See **THE SIN OF EXPOSITION**}

This is only the barest minimum of what dialogue can do, entire books are written on the subject. This is among the most misunderstood and underdeveloped areas. You need to devote a good deal of research to this skill. [see **Recommended Texts in Appendices**]

---

* People who are being dishonest or playing with the truth often speak in clichés.

FINDING YOUR VOICES

Listening and borrowing from the real spoken world

Here we need to acknowledge that, at different times in our lives, we have talked in different ways and used key phrases and mannerisms.

As writers, we need to become very observant of how different people speak. Language is governed by gender, age, race, nationality, education, peer group, economic demographic and region and whether it is your native tongue.

People from cities often speak differently than their country cousins. Working class people will speak differently to upper class people. Racial dialects and patois are particular to specific ethnic groups. Educated people will speak differently to those with less education.

Children speak differently from teenagers, who again speak differently than those in their twenties and thirties. They then are different to middle aged people, if only slightly. But often elderly people have very specific turns of phrase that hark back to an era when those sayings were spoken. Often, they use phrases that now sound quaint- from another age.

Keep a pocket notebook to jot down different ways of speaking. Make notes that will help create characters' voices. Really listen to those around and grab their phrases to help you build dialogue.

DIFFERENTIATING PRINCIPAL CHARACTERS

To every character a distinctive voice - identifying how and why people, and hence characters, speak the way they do

Where principal characters are going to have conversations, it is helpful for each of them to have specific personalities that are evident in their ways of speaking.

READERS SHOULD BE ABLE TO IDENTIFY WHO IS SPEAKING BY THEIR TONE AND CHARACTER, WITHOUT TOO MUCH IDENTIFICATION i.e. 'said Tom', 'said Anjie'.

As a reader, we begin to know who said what, by the way they said it.

The three main characters of the *'Harry Potter'* series – Harry, Ron and Hermione have very specific ways of talking that are in keeping with their characters. How would you describe them? Look at passages from the books and identify their conversation styles.

This is not an easy thing to achieve and when you first begin all or many of your characters will sound the same. Becoming aware of that is the first step to rectifying it.

Having backstory that fleshes out your characters will help you to find mannerism, patterns of speech and stylistic approaches to the way your characters will speak.

CHAPTER FIVE
DEEPER STORY STRUCTURE

The Story Arc
The Character Arc
Who or what is driving this story? Plot or Character Driven Stories
Subplots
P.O.V. and the Fourth Wall First, Second and Third Person Narratives

THE STORY ARC

From Once Upon a Time to [Not so] Happily Ever After and all that's in-between ONLY MUCH BIGGER

The story arc is the overall blueprint of where a story goes. The Story Arc encompasses the themes, the action, the character development, the plot points and turning points {including climaxes and revelations}. In complex stories this will involve many characters and incidents. Within the Story

Arc are a number of Character Arcs both small and large. Each main character, whether positive or negative, will have a character arc that fits into the whole scheme of things.

As an example – The seven books of the *'Harry Potter'* series have a Story Arc that appears to begin with the death of Harry's parents and the arrival of their one-year old child at the Dursleys', even though the story opens with Harry approaching his eleventh birthday. And ends with the defeat of Harry's parent's murderer Lord Voldemort; leaving Harry and his friends free to grow up and have families of their own.

By virtue of flashback, it goes back to the first meeting of Tom Riddle and Albus Dumbledore. But no, it goes back to Albus Dumbledore's youth and the accidental killing of his sister. And if we go to the telling of the ancient tale of 'The Deathly Hallows' it seems to be lost in mythic times.

As we can see this is a huge story arc. And within this are the character arcs of many people, each with secrets and desires, fears and burdens to bear. I will look briefly at a character arc within the larger story arc, as part of the next section.

IDEAS FOR SITUATIONS AND CHARACTERS WILL COME TO YOU SPONTANEOUSLY BUT AT SOME STAGE YOU WILL NEED TO PLACE THEM INTO A STORY ARC.

THE CHARACTER ARC

From negative to positive and from positive to negative

In every story, we go on a journey both externally and internally. We travel to places but equally we travel inside our character's hearts and minds.

For a story to be satisfying to the reader it must have an emotional core- that is the characters we identify with {including the negative ones} must have an emotional, psychological and maybe even a spiritual journey.

Sometimes that journey is one of self-realisation and positivity; sometimes it is one of loss, failure and negativity.

The Character Arc is sometimes called the **Arc of Transformation**, meaning it reveals how a character changes or transforms.

Heroes and villains, participants and observers can all have character arcs. They begin here but they end up there, hopefully wiser and happier but not always.

Obviously, the main character[s] will be the one[s] with the most pronounced character arc. And that arc will relate solidly to the Story Arc and main theme.

Often, they will go from failure to success, from heartlessness and cruelty to kindness, love and acceptance, from rags to riches, from novice to master, from ignorance to knowledge and from obscurity to recognition- to name just some of the developments a character can go through.

Reversals of fortune are just as interesting. They can happen for main characters or secondary ones, for heroes or villains and for positive or negative characters. We watch this trajectory with fascination, as characters go from riches to ruin, from normality to confusion and distress, from power to powerlessness and from being adored to being rejected. Some characters who succeed in the end will be required to fail and reach rock bottom part way through the story – so a fall and then a rise. Still others involve a rise and fall and rise again.

This then is what a character arc does. Let's look at a particular character arc within the larger Story Arc.

Severus Snape appears throughout the first few books as a villainous character, with a pathological hatred of Harry. But as the story opens up, and we go further back into the lives of previous students of Hogwarts, we begin to see that things are not what they appear.

Let us trace the life of Severus Snape and see the character arc he has.

As a child, he is something of a misfit but has been befriended by the beautiful girl Lily. They both head off to school, where he becomes the target of cruel bullying by James Potter and his friends.

He has not been able to declare how he feels about Lily and is deeply embittered when she becomes romantically involved, with his archenemy James Potter.

It is at this point that Severus begins to dabble in dark magic and comes under the influence of Tom Riddle. Years pass and Riddle, now transformed into the powerful Lord Voldemort, is obsessed with omnipotence and immortality. When the prophecy of "a boy child born to defeat Voldemort" is revealed, he seeks out James and Lily Potter and their new born.

Desperate to save her, Severus confides in Albus Dumbledore but fails to keep Lily safe. Consumed with grief, he vows to protect the child of his great love. Part of this vow is to do with a debt he owes to James Potter for saving his life but the love he felt for Lily is surely the driving force in his protective mission.

But on Harry's arrival at Hogwarts, Severus is unable to see Harry's true worth. All he sees is a reminder of the torment he suffered at the hands of the father and misjudges all of Harry's actions, as being as wilful and conceited as James'. And yet he keeps faith with his promise to both the memory of Lily and to Dumbledore, to protect Harry. He works as a double agent. He sits at the right hand of Lord Voldemort and feeds information back to Dumbledore.

Even after he kills Dumbledore, things are not as they seem. Later we find that Dumbledore is dying and Snape's act was not murder but a mercy killing.

But this mercy killing will cost Severus his life when Voldemort seeks ultimate power, as the possessor of the 'Elder Wand'. Dying, Snape tells Harry to take his memories and use them to reveal the final truth about his role in saving Harry and hopefully defeating Voldemort.

When Harry finally understands, he defeats Voldemort and nineteen years later the reader discovers that he has honoured his long dead teacher, by giving one of his children the name Albus Severus. This is an extraordinary and beautifully satisfying character arc. It has irony and nobility and subtly revealed secrets that take hold of the reader and surprise and surprise throughout the story arc.

{See also **PAY OFFS/ TWISTS AND RIDDLES** and **IRONY CHAPTER EIGHT**}

The character arc is directly connected to the plotline and the plot points and each significant turning point in the story. Plotlines, plot points and turning points are discussed in Chapter Eight.

Having established the direction the main character will take in your story you need to decide how you will tell the story- That is, will the story be told from the viewpoint of the protagonist or by a narrator or a mixture of both? Will it be in 1st, 2nd or 3rd person?

{See P.O.V. and The Fourth Wall This Chapter}

WHO IS DRIVING THIS STORY?

What is the engine of your story? Plot or character driven stories

Stories can begin in many ways. While action and incidents can and are integral to any story, they are the driving force behind only some narratives.

PLOT-DRIVEN STORY

In its simplest definition, a Plot is a sequence of actions and events that tell a story- in other words a storyline. A plot driven story means an action driven story

While the focal character may grow and change this is essentially a story built around upheavals, dangers and threats. The main character may and probably does have character defects but it is how he or she overcomes these, when **numerous and powerful outside forces act upon him or her, that is the operating principle** here. *'Robinson Crusoe'* by Daniel Defoe is an example of this, as are most comic and graphic novels.

Or the main character is resolute and immutable and we watch as this powerful figure conquers his or her adversaries. This is of course the 'superhero' motif. This can be found in *'Viking myths'* and *'Sherlock Holmes'*.

CHARACTER-DRIVEN STORY

This is a story in which the main protagonist has a series of internal struggles and character traits that will dictate the way the story goes. Outside events will have an influence but the focal character's **inner desires, fears, obsessions are the driving force.** *'The Picture of Dorian Gray'* by Oscar Wilde is one such example and the Guy De Maupassant story *'The Necklace'* is another. And of course, the extraordinary *'Madame Bovary'* by Gustave Flaubert.

Writers in this form create characters and then devise flaws within them that are large enough to drive the narrative.

TAUTOLOGY

Plot and story are sometimes used to mean the same thing and this can be confusing. Be aware of this. Some people use the expression a character driven plot but then will say a plot driven story. You wouldn't say a plot driven plot. This sounds ridiculous but it does mean an action driven story – a story in which plot {actions and incidents} is the operating principle.

In the end, most stories have a mixture of both character and action driven scenarios.

SUB PLOTS

Don't forget the little guys in the story

It is easy to become engrossed in the main story and the main character arc and not fully resolve your secondary characters. You have set up the needs and desires of these characters also.

So, allow your readers to follow these characters to their natural conclusions, as well. If you have set up needs and desires, failures and humiliations, how will the companions resolve these? To fail to fully realize your companions, allies, villains – all secondary characters - is to seriously reduce the validity of the world you have created.

One method, of making sure that they all reach their appropriate ends, is to create backstories for all and to set each one out as part of your treatment. {see **Treatment Chapter Eight**}.

Make sure they come to completion in your first draft {see **The Next Steps Chapter Eight**}. You can improve or change smaller character arcs in later drafts but from the start get them down on screen or paper, so that they are not forgotten.

P.O.V. AND THE FOURTH WALL

Whose story is this anyway? 1st, 2nd and 3rd person / Choices of which person you write in

These terms relate to how you focus a narrative; that is the choices you make in the way you tell the story. These terms are from the performing and cinema arts and focus on how an audience sees the unfolding drama.

P.O.V. is shorthand for Point of View, which in filmmaking is when we, as an audience, see the world through the eyes of a character – from their point of view, through the lens of the camera. In other words, when the camera chooses to show only what would be seen through one person's eyes and dictates that you are now inside the story, seeing the limited worldview of that character.

The Fourth Wall is a term that comes from the theatre and imagines the stage as a room with two side walls [wings] and a back wall. The fourth wall is the audience, who are watching the whole scene from their seats. This position is sometimes called being 'the fly on the wall', since you are observing the story but are not part of it.

As writers, we can and do utilize a mixture of both. There are moments within a novel where we need to tell our story from one person's viewpoint and other times when we will be the outside observer of a group scene or we observe the actions of a single individual.

If you watch a film you will see the camera choices that the director has made. Sometimes these are point of view shots and other times they are wide shots or two shots in which we are observing from outside- a silent observer, a fly on the wall.

As the author, you not only make these same sorts of decisions as to what your audience, the readership will have revealed to them/what they will see but you also choose what person narrates the story.

Films are told from various viewpoints but by virtue of what they choose to show, they are First person when P.O.V. and Third person when we watch the scene as an outside observer, often in a wide shot.

You have these choices also and will move between these different positions. You can tell your stories in First, Second or Third person but even in these there are various forms.

NARRATIVE POSITIONS AND THEIR ADVANTAGES

First person involves the story being narrated, to you the reader, from one person's viewpoint using 'I' and 'me' and when they are accompanied 'we'. That is, the character is a participant in the story - the main character, for example, Gulliver in *'Gulliver's Travels'* by Jonathan Swift. This is a series of fantastical adventures told as it appears and happens to him and told by him. 'He' or 'She' is always another character speaking to the main character, who is telling the story, e.g. 'I found him most discourteous. He always spoke to me in condescending tones!' 'They' will be others discussed by the main character.

Sometimes the story is told from a secondary character's point of view who observes and comments on the main protagonist but is also involved in the action.

Dr Watson is one example of this and here the choice of this once-removed narrator is clear. Like the audience, Dr Watson needs to be baffled by the crime and astounded by Sherlock Holmes' ability to solve the seemingly inexplicable. Sherlock reveals his solution to the doctor and by extension to us. What was unfathomable is shown to be obvious through the powers of observation and deduction. The doctor marvels, we marvel and he replies, *'Elementary, my dear Watson'*.

Some narrators are supplementary characters who tell the story from a distance, such as Nick Carraway in *'The Great Gatsby'*. Often this involves some level of detachment or bittersweet irony.

Some are 'Frame Narrators' who tell a story of others. In Emily Bronte's *'Wuthering Heights'* events are revealed via a visitor, who has been told these incidents by the Linton family housekeeper. The main characters are placed in the narrative of 'Wuthering Heights' by these outside observers.

Second Person narrative voice is reasonably rare. It requires a story to be told in which 'you' are the protagonist. It refers to the reader as 'you' within the story. For an example of how this works read **'The Power of the Orphan'**. Here I have purposefully put you the reader, as the chief observer of events in the story. Although the story is about your friend it is your reactions and your relationship to them that is central to the story. *'If On A Winter's Night A Traveller'* by Italo Calvino is a fabulous example of second person narrative that plays with the construction of stories and takes its readers into altered realities.

Third Person narrative voice is the most common means of telling stories and provides the greatest flexibility for the author.

Here the story can be told from numerous perspectives and each one will be referred to as 'he', 'she' and 'they' or by their given names for example Elizabeth Bennett. The narrator is outside the story, as an observer but is often in an almost god-like position. That is, they are able to reveal to the audience what individual characters think and feel as well as their dialogue and actions.

Third Person Choices

As the narrator, you will make decisions about what a character will know or learn throughout a story. What a character knows or learns is what is by turn revealed to an audience.

Limited Narrator

This is where the narrator knows and tells all there is about a single character, usually the main character but the rest of the story is closed to them. So, we see the main character live out their life in much the same way that we live out ours – that is, stumbling through, discovering as we go.

They will tell a story in which the main character will travel through the events and will gradually arrive at answers. Truths will be searched for and mysteries unravelled but only in the fullness of time. The main character, and by extension the readership, will be equally in the dark and come to conclusions together. They will travel in linear time and stay within the here and now.

This is useful in crime fiction and horror stories but can just as easily be used to gradually reveal a hidden and often unpleasant truth in emotive realist fiction. Once you have decided to write in this limited way, that is you have established this sort of relationship with the reader, you don't tend to deviate from it. You cannot describe things that are unknown to the focal character, ahead of them discovering them, in the story arc. We must arrive at incident and revelation together. Limited Narrator can be told in 1st, 2nd or 3rd person.

Omniscient Narrator

The narrator here can and does work with many characters and reveals a number of viewpoints. This narrator travels to any time or place to continue the story. The author has equal access to the thoughts, actions and desires of all characters. This does not mean that he or she will reveal what each character is doing or what their actions mean all at once. They still make choices to reveal story and character motivation in a gradual fashion. We still want to read a story that intrigues but this kind of narrator has a wider range to draw on. The author is like a master puppeteer who manipulates each character in the service of the story. This kind of story telling is often used in large sagas where there is often the broad sweep of history. Leo Tolstoy's *'War and Peace'* is an example of this. James Clavell's *'Shogun'* is another example.

Novels will often move between these two approaches. We can keep our main character in the dark and force them to discover truth by degrees and we will only be as informed as they are, at any point in the book. Or we can move away from our main character from time to time and be made aware of other peoples' lives. This puts us into a position of knowing more than our main protagonist. We watch to see if they will catch up to us or if they will choose the right path towards truth or fall by the wayside.

Unreliable Narrator

This is a story in which we buy into how the narrative unfolds and at a certain point in the telling we realize that we have been fooled.

That in fact, the reality we have accepted is false and things are not what they appear or at the very least that there is more than one interpretation of how the story has been told. *'The Life of Pi'* is a very clever example of this, in which the characters of animals may well be illusory and those animals hide a much darker and less palatable reality, that the protagonist/narrator cannot come to terms with. Another example of this is *'The Magus'* by John Fowles - a story of various realities that are not what they appear and that torment the main character.

CHAPTER SIX
DEEPER QUESTIONS AND APPROACHES

Title, Prologue and Opening Scene
What is at Stake?
The Power of the Orphan
Themes
The Truth is out there
The Two Taboos
Resonance
Exercise 13
The Emotional Core
Conflict
Exercise 14
Conflict and the Emotional Core –A Symbiotic relationship
Write about What You Know

TITLE, PROLOGUE AND OPENING SCENES

When we begin the begin

TITLE

In the way that names of characters and places create very definite images and impressions the same can be said of titles. The title is the first point of entry into the story- it can create mystery, intrigue, can set mood, define character or setting. Finally, it is shorthand for the sort of story to be told. It is a selling point for your audience – they know what they are getting.

Below are some evocative titles that tell us a good deal about what is going to unfold.

Great Expectations

The Call of the Wild

Brave New World

Stranger in a Strange Land

The Great Gatsby

To Kill a Mockingbird

Gone with the Wind

The Grapes of Wrath

Heart of Darkness

Something Wicked This Way Comes

Alice's Adventures in Wonderland

PROLOGUE

Some tales travel straight into character, setting and action while others will use a prologue to set up vital information or mood.

Prologue orients an audience. It will set scenes, illuminate characters, reveal the beginnings of a mystery, introduce a hero or villain, create the back history that informs the current situation or create a series of unanswered questions that will be the backbone of the tale about to be told.

Not all stories require a prologue. Often the choice of a prologue is dictated by the amount or intricacy of the information in the set up.

If you can get away with not using a prologue, that can be to your advantage. If you can reveal information gradually throughout the Acts, using dialogue, character and situation, then a prologue will be unnecessary.

The choice to use a prologue is a very deliberate one. Many writers abhor prologues as they have the effect of distancing the reader initially from character and incident. It is often seen as lazy or poorly constructed writing. Elmore Leonard says never use a prologue but as a crime writer there isn't much call for that. Other types of writing may need one.

OPENING SCENE

Not every story will begin with a prologue but they all have an opening scene. Much thought needs to be given to this.

Do we begin close to the event or action that sets our story rolling?

Do we build up gradually to give our audience the tone of our story?

How much is your story dependent on place?

Are character relationships what we want to reveal first and the setting is revealed as a secondary aspect?

How much is it dependent on mood? Such as the psychological build up in the opening chapters of *'Dracula'* by Bram Stoker.

Perhaps the nature of the main character needs to be revealed quickly?

Perhaps revealed slowly?

> For instance, the two main characters Bathsheba and Gabriel from *'Far from the Madding Crowd'* by Thomas Hardy notice one another. This begins with a brief encounter on a country road but being both proud and independent they move on. It is some time before they are involved with each other again. By which time we have begun to discern their differing personalities and finally they have a greater appreciation of each other.

These are all questions that must to be asked and weighed up before you begin. Opening scenes make a promise to the reader that the story will lead somewhere and that the journey will be worth it.

And when you ask these questions you need to ask the question that the author must know of their story, right from the beginning. Even if the readership will not know it till later and that is…

WHAT IS AT STAKE?

What physically and emotionally hangs in the balance – the core of your story

This question centres on the emotional core/on the central conflict and on the character and story arcs. It is the question that allows you to state your story in one or two synoptic sentences and to identify your theme. {see **THEMES**}. We deal with this in a coming section. I mention it here because 'what is at stake?' has a major influence on how you design your story and how you build that opening scene.

THE POWER OF THE ORPHAN

From Cinderella to Cosette in Les Miserables - Why the orphan reoccurs in literature?

What do all these characters have in common, Superman, Batman, Spiderman, Cinderella, Oliver Twist, James from James and the Giant Peach, Harry Potter?

Why is the Orphan such a useful and powerful figure in literature?

Imagine you live in a small village in central Europe, provincial China or on the plains of Africa. Where doesn't matter as this story belongs to us all.

You are ten, eleven perhaps twelve and your best friend is of a similar age.

One day you return home from the well or the day's hunt or with your bundle of firewood and there is your friend locked out of their house. The door is barred and your friend is screaming, wailing, bashing on the outside desperate to enter.

All of the village folk stand at a distance and watch. None intervene.

You step forward but a look from those around you says, 'do not interfere!'

A night and a day go by as your friend lies in the doorway, curled up like a street dog, making eye contact with no-one.

On the fourth day, the village elders gather. Behind them stand too burly men with burning torches. The oldest of the men pulls your friend aside and then the two strong men breach the door. The moment it opens they quickly step back. For a long while no-one moves, then resignedly the old man slowly enters. The stench of disease and death wafts from the broken doorway. Your friend stands frozen, eyes fixed on the entrance.

The old man steps out and shakes his head and with great haste the two men step forward, brandishing their torches.

A great piercing cry, like a wounded animal, rises up but your friend does not fall. Instead her body is rigid, locked into the bitter knowledge that all is gone. Soon her world will be ashes. For the next few days the girl lives by the town well. Some of the villagers have left food but that dwindles to nothing. It has been a hard winter and the summer harvest was meagre.

You are still forbidden to speak to her but you watch her from afar. Once and only once, she makes eye contact with you but she too knows that everything has changed forever.

On the eighth day, you wake and walk to the well with your bucket. She is not there. The spot where she slept in the dust shows many footprints.

You will never see her again.

Family is our shelter, our provider, our comforter in times of distress, our teacher and our protector. To lose family is probably our most deep-seated fear and this makes 'The Orphan' an extremely potent force within a narrative.

THEMES

The one to two sentence Synopsis and the Main and Secondary themes

What do I want to say in my story? What is my story all about? Does it have a moral or a life lesson? This does not have to be preachy. In fact, it is better if what you are trying to get across is presented subtly. Often the way to clarify what your story is about is by asking yourself this.

"*Can I tell the reader what my story is about in one or two sentences?*"

If I can, I will be getting close to identifying its' theme.

Though a story will have a main theme, it can and often does have secondary themes. But discovering a theme or themes is often what happens after your story has arrived. In the throes of creating a story you put it all down and then the themes start to appear to you. Sometimes as you write, sometimes when you finish.

Here are some single sentence descriptions of well-known stories and their main themes.

CINDERELLA – An orphan girl faces trials but through a kind fairy finds love and prosperity. **THEME** – *Love wins in the end.*

KING MIDAS – A King is granted the power to change all he touches into gold but soon discovers that it is his undoing. **THEME** – *Greed destroys.*

ROMEO AND JULIET - Two teenagers, from opposing families, fall in love. The hatred the two families have for each other eventually claims the young lovers' lives. **THEME**- *Bigotry and hatred destroy love.*

Notice that the theme tends to relate to how the story ends. The story arc and the plotline will arrive at this very same place.

In *'Romeo and Juliet'* we see a conclusion where the two lovers pay with their lives. Those left behind must deal with the tragedy. For them and us the theme is clear. Hatred has killed love and we must all learn to transcend this.

Once you have reduced your story down to a sentence or two your main theme stands revealed. You can then go back and see if your character arcs and your Story Arc fulfil that Theme. You look at your secondary themes in the same way.

TO BE ABLE TO STATE THE STORY IN ONE OR TWO SENTENCES AND YOUR THEME IN A SHORT STATEMENT, WILL GIVE YOU THE GIFT OF REAL FOCUS.

Sometimes you will write out your story and be unaware of what your theme is, till you have finished. This is just the nature of 'The Muse'. It is only when you go back and reread or rework it that you begin to see a theme has appeared. This is particularly true of short stories. Novels and sagas will often have large and readily identifiable themes. However even some of these larger stories may not reveal their themes till the Second Draft.

Here are some of the Universal Themes that appear constantly in contemporary literature. Some will be used as Main themes and others as Secondary themes within a story.

COMMON UNIVERSAL THEMES

PERSONAL GROWTH	SOCIETY AND INDIVIDUALISM
The Power of Compassion	Skill versus Strength
Self-reliance	Social Class
Childish Parents and Mature Children	Secrecy
Coming of Age and Rites of Passage	The Power of Language
Discovering Who You Are	Past versus Present
Dreams and What They Mean	The American Dream?
Bereavement and Loss	What is a Family in the 21st Century?
Loss of Innocence	Loss of Reputation and the Road Back
Self-Improvement and Ambition	The Power of Storytelling
Temptation	Isolation
Mental Disorders/ Psychological Problems	Interracial Relationships
Crime and the Guilty Mind	Civilization vs. Tribalism

Loyalty
Finding the Hero Within
The Black Dog of Depression
Anorexia and Bulimia
Anger and its' Legacy
The Rocky Road to Love
Family and the Need to Belong
Abandonment
Forgiveness
Establishing Personal Identity
Dealing with Tragedy
Personal Rivalry
Lost Hopes and Dreams

Pride and Arrogance
Beauty and Vanity
Living in Fear
Envy and Jealousy

Personal Conspiracy
The Nobility of Self- Sacrifice
Obsession
Self-Deception
Friendship
Drug Abuse
Parenthood
Sexuality
Alcohol Abuse
Struggles within a Family
Divorce

Crime and Punishment
Injustice and the Underdog
Dangerous Secrets
Inhumanity
Racial Discrimination
Immigrants in a New World
Intolerance

Women in Society
Class Struggle
Identity within Society
The Nature of Evil
The Denial of Truth
The Dead and their Influence on the Living
Duty and Honour
Striving for Freedom
The Search for Truth
The Power of the Written Word
Deceit and its' Repercussions
Suspicious Minds
Political Conspiracy
Deceptive Appearances
Greed
Alienation
Bullying
Traditions and Customs
The Power of Education
Poverty and Social Dislocation
Nationalism both Positive and Negative

Traditional Values
The Effects of Violence
Suicide and its Impact

THE MEANING OF LIFE
Death and What Lies Beyond?
Faith and Doubt
Memory and Recollection

The Quest for Happiness
Destiny
Home
Community
Death and Rebirth
Life's Regrets
Spirituality
The Value of Work
Money and Influence

FATE AND CHANCE
Betrayal

The Innocent Victim
Survival in a Hostile Environment
Natural Catastrophe
Man Made Catastrophe
The Quest
The Chase
The Power of the Supernatural
In the Hands of Fate
The Forces of Nature

SECONDARY THEMES

Any number of lesser but still important themes can and do run through well-developed stories. The Main Theme of the *Harry Potter* series is, I believe, 'The Power of Love- to save, to heal, and to transform.' It is 'Love' that protects Harry when Voldemort seeks him out as a young child. It is 'Love' [for Lily] that binds Snape to Harry till his own demise. It is 'Love' of his friends that persuades Harry to face his enemy; even though he is convinced he will die. It is 'Love' that Voldemort scoffs at in their final encounter. But there are many other themes running through the saga, for example:

Racism and Discrimination.   Friendship   Self Belief
Self-Sacrifice   The importance of family

Notice how these secondary themes can and do relate to the main theme. This is often the case. Secondary themes are rarely at variance with the main theme.

Questions to ask yourself as you design your story and build around your theme.

Will it be recognisable?

Can you easily state it?

Can the theme be expressed as a well-known universal truth, such as 'To the victor go the spoils' or 'Time waits for no one' or 'Only love can break your heart?'

Is your theme one that an audience will relate to and care about?

Is it a universal theme that will matter to an audience anywhere?

Will it grab the attention of an audience?

THE TRUTH IS OUT THERE

What is truth in fiction and where do we find it?

Robert Bloch the brilliant science fiction writer said 'Wells, Huxley and Orwell can still enthral today, despite dated references and failed prophecies, because their concepts and characters are endowed with timeless truths that endure'

Here is the most elusive aspect of writing of them all – finding truth. By this I don't simply mean facts. Truth may be built around facts, embedded in believable realities {however unusual} but it is something other than that.

You know when you watch a film or read a book if it has that intangible truth. You also know when it is missing; when a story is contrived and has no centre, no internal belief, hope, desire or revelation.

Truth is something deep, it has something to do with heart and emotions but for all that it is not a romantic notion. You know when it is missing and you know when it is there.

Truth in a story involves searching. The story may not have answers but it will certainly ask questions; questions about existence.

What are we doing here?

How do we make sense of our world?

How do we resist the powers that govern our lives?

Can we find deep profound love?

We ask questions about our society and fundamentally about ourselves.

Truth is a search for love and again I am not talking hearts and flowers. We all begin our lives as infants and toddlers, utterly dependent on parents for food, affection, protection and approval.

As we grow we transfer these needs and desires, to a larger world of school, teachers and peers. Later we will transfer those same {it is always the same} needs and desires to our lovers and our community. But always we are seeking those same things- love, protection, approval and acceptance.

A search for truth in a story is a search for these things but it is also an attempt to investigate what our world does to prevent us from finding those things.

Those include-

Dystopian societies

Dysfunctional families.

Punitive tyrants and power wielders

Life/freedom denying attitudes

Fundamentalist theologies and ideologies

The handicaps we all acquire or inherit that prevent us from fully functioning and finding love, acceptance and self-knowledge.

Stories are always about identity and existence - who we are and how we fit or don't fit in to our society/reality/loving relationships. Even your smallest story will ask these questions – they will be part of the quest, the conflict and the emotional core. In larger stories, they will be more pronounced, often appearing in thoughts and conversations.

Truth is, in the end, individual for both the writer and their characters. But we must ask these questions of ourselves and our story creations.

THE BIG QUESTION

I have not mentioned a search for the higher truths.

Do we have a purpose?

Do we believe in the existence of a Creator?

Do we believe in an interventionist God?

These are philosophical questions and may well work in an essay or a sermon but do they work in a narrative?

They can but they have to be deeply embedded in the storyline, otherwise they become somewhat preachy and detract from the story itself. If you do have a belief system you wish to impart to your audience, then you need to be subtle. C.S. Lewis created a series of books that carry deeply Christian concepts in *'The Chronicles of Narnia'* but the story was paramount. You can enjoy the stories for their own sake and many readers have read them, without realizing their allegorical nature.

THE TWO TABOOS

Sex and Death – not in front of the children

In Western society, the two taboos that are suppressed, not talked about, feared, obsessed over and used to control people are sex and death. In other words, the 'truths' we are preoccupied with but fear and deny.

These two aspects of humanity need to be appreciated and explored as they are the two elements of our psyche that exercise some of the most powerful influences on our behaviour. While they may not be the theme of your narrative they lay below the surface of character behaviours.

Before we reach puberty, as young children, we begin to inquire about ourselves and others' similarities and differences. We begin to acknowledge and sometimes physically explore the differences between us. Reaching puberty with the rise of our hormones, we begin a process of attraction for the same or the opposite sex; one that informs our behaviour until the end of our lives. This is both a natural force designed to keep the generations going and/or a desire to bond with others to help us get through our lives.

Sexual desire melded with a need for love, recognition and acceptance make a very potent concoction. It is the driving force of our existence.

But, and here is the important but for us as writers – it is a force that we only partially understand and try as we might we do not have a great deal of control over it. The characters within our stories can be obsessed, driven mad, manipulated, elated, despairing and denied, due to the power of sex, desire and love. This primal force is the major underlying driver of narratives - one that readers will identify with.

The other force that we all contend with is death. Here also our childhood experiences teach us of the impermanence of the world around us as people, animals, members of our family all die. As we grow to maturity we begin to come to terms with our own mortality. Our narratives will reflect various aspects of our relationship with death – dread, immense sorrow, fascination, foreboding and perhaps, as the years progress a growing knowledge and acceptance.

The denial of sex and death are ways in which characters are controlled within a narrative by repressive forces – the Church, the State, the ruling class, dystopian societies, brutal inhibited parents and so on.

All this is 'grist for the mill' for a writer. These natural elements are potent story starters and drivers and we need to be aware of them, know them, study them and utilize them within our narratives.

RESONANCE

The moments in your writing where an audience recognizes life as we know it

Not all truth is profound. Writers also find small moments of truth as well.

Good writers create descriptions of people and settings and situations that ring true for an audience, even if that description is not part of the reader's firsthand experience. The reader will still recognize it as 'real life'. Sometimes they can be quite small but revealing vignettes.

'She was dressed in a soft cream gown that flowed to the ground and a figure hugging bodice that seemed to be held up

by magic. I looked across at my daughter as we walked, in a stately gate, down the aisle of well-wishers. She gripped my arm and gave a small sideways glance as if to say, 'We have finally arrived at the moment I wished for.'

Then I looked ahead, determined to fulfil my one small duty with all the care and gentleness I could muster.

At the end of the aisle stood the groom, who never once looked at me or the hundred or more friends and family. His eyes never left her, as she approached and in those brief few seconds I knew that everything would be alright.

They would have trials and hardships and yes even heartache but they would have each other and that would be enough to carry them through.'

You may not be a father or a bride or groom but all of us have been to weddings and seen this look shared between two lovers, at their moment of commitment. This is **'a moment taken from real life'** and like this passage you must find these kinds of moments in your writing.

Sometimes they can be no more than a couple of words, a single description, a phrase describing a look or a feeling, a sentence or a paragraph that captures a mood, a shared understanding, a moment of realization or revelation, - **'a truth within the moment'**.

This is one of the profound challenges you have as a writer and requires you to be very observant and more importantly to commit those observations to paper or file and to know when to use them in your writing. To find those things **'that resonate.'**

EXERCISE 13

Take a moment from your life and turn it into a brief passage. Choose one that was illuminating for you. Capture the essential truth of it. You can choose any moment from any period of your life.

Here are others you might like to choose from.

- A moment with one of your parents.
- That first connection with someone you were attracted to.
- When you decided to walk out of a painful and pointless situation and not look back.
- The moment you were watching someone who didn't know you were and they revealed something about themselves by their actions.
- A moment where a truth about yourself was revealed to you.

THE EMOTIONAL CORE

The single most important element of your storytelling and how it goes hand in hand with Conflict

This is the most important section of the lot. I was tempted to put this all in UPPER CASE and in RED. But no, just take it to heart...

Writers make choices. You choose what you want to tell, what you want to reveal. You choose what you want an audience to experience.

A truly moving story is not merely one that has a series of events/dangers /challenges constructed from the appropriate story building blocks. To achieve a story that really moves a reader we need to have **AN EMOTIONAL CORE.**

The principal character needs to be within a story that will cost them emotionally and because we identify with them it will cost us also.

They need to experience the pain and joy, the terror and exhilaration of **living deeply.** They must have something significant to lose and something significant to gain.

Surface stories, that rely on action and events only, will ultimately be unsatisfactory to the reader. You need much more. Create storylines that not only put our characters in danger but also put them into situations where they are in emotional turmoil - where they have something emotional and psychological to lose.

Where they are misunderstood or misrepresented.

Where they have been lied to and cheated on.

Where their need for love has been denied.

Where their need for recognition and acceptance has been denied.

Where their rights and their freedoms have been taken away.

Where they face great and heartbreaking loss.

Where injustice is felt and incenses an audience.

The emotional subtext of great stories is the main reason that audiences identify with them. No matter how exciting the dangers and events are, **it is the heart of the story that matters**

THIS TAKES TIME- For an audience to feel the pain and longing of a character WE MUST KNOW THE CHARACTER.

We travel with the characters and grow to love and care for them- then and only then will failures and successes tug at our hearts.

You now have story ideas, story structure, characters, backstory, character arcs and themes and hopefully an emotional core. But this is not enough for an action story- one in which the characters face and overcome challenges. For this we need the magic ingredient-CONFLICT.

CONFLICT

Why life is better when you are chased by a sabre tooth tiger

HOWEVER

Not all stories are reliant on extreme conflict

Some stories are observations of a time and place, while others are a recollection of an event or a character. They often have a wistful almost dreamlike aura. They are pleasant to read and can be very beautiful and well written but they usually carry within them some small agitation; something that acts to increase the tension in the story. But they are not action stories and they do not put their characters into life threatening or life changing situations. The beautiful book *'Cider with Rosie'* by Laurie Lee is a good example of this kind of writing.

Having recognized them, let us move on and deal with the risky stuff.

'Action Stories' do rely on extreme conflict.

'GARK'S STORY'

'Not long after we climbed down out of the trees and stood upright on the plains of Africa, Gark and Sarz sat across from each other around the campfire. And this is the story that

Gark told.

You did not know me then, my beautiful wife. This was before you came to the tribe, when my life was only seventeen rainy seasons.

We were a hunting and gathering tribe of fourteen men and twenty-three women with children. Our leader was a powerful man called Rak who would control both the hunt and who could have partners in the tribe.

What Rak most feared was not the huge sabre-toothed Tigers that roamed the grassland but the young, strong men who grew up within the tribe. His fear was that one day, one would challenge him and take his place.

But Rak had been lucky because one by one the strongest of the men had all died. They had gone out on the hunt in the early hours of the morning and by the following night they were dead. Almost always they were slain by the tiger that we were hunting. Only the weaker men remained and they followed Rak's every command.

For some weeks now Rak had been watching me, as I grew into manhood. He watched me play with the other boys, he watched me race and win and he watched as I carved weapons and threw them.

And I watched him watching me.

One night, after the fire had burned down to embers, I saw a shadow moving on the edge of the encampment. It was a hot summer night and I slept in the open, with very few furs on. The animal skins that covered my body during the day lay hanging on the branch of a balboa tree.

The shadow came closer and slowly I reached out for my knife, ready to fight off this intruder. But he did not come to me. Instead the shadow moved to my clothing and began to rub something onto the skins. He was there for no more than a few seconds and then he was gone back into the darkness.

I gathered up some dry grass into my eating bowl and placed two or three red coals in among them. When I came to my skins I blew hard and the fire took hold. The grass burnt quickly but in those few moments I saw all I needed to know. My skins were covered in animal blood and it would be dried on by morning...............'

Conflict is essential to an action story.

EXERCISE 14.

Take all the threads of this story and create an ending. Write your own conclusion using these questions as a guide.
    What has been set up here?
    Who is the shadow?
    What does Rak intend for Gark?
    How could the blood on his garments achieve this?
    Is there some way that Gark can turn the tables on Rak?
    When do you think the climax of this conflict/story will occur?
    He has lived to tell the tale so how did he achieve this?
    Consider all these elements and work out how events could work in Gark's favour.

Note: My version of the end is at the conclusion of the section. Do not look at it. Instead try to figure out what would work for you.

Not all conflict is physical as in 'Gark's Story'. Sometimes it is psychological and the force you must contend with is yourself. There is probably no better example of this than Edgar Allan Poe's *'The Tell-Tale Heart'*.

Read this and watch the gradual rise in tension; the rise in internal conflict. Look at how Poe achieves this.

Conflict requires opposing forces. Often that can be the opposing intentions of the two main adversaries. They both seek the same goal- the girl, the boy, fame, fortune, the position of power and privilege. Sometimes the forces that face each other have an ideological bent - differences of religion, world view, and political viewpoint, the restoration of law and order versus anarchy and crime. Other times the opposing forces can be tribal, nationalist, racist or just plain hungry i.e. the opposing force simply sees the hero as dinner.

Questions that you need to ask yourself when creating a story and looking at the central issue of conflict include -

Does it have real conflict?

What kind of conflict is it, physical or psychological or a mix of both?

Is the conflict sustained?

Is it believable/compelling/worth investing in?

CONCLUSION TO - Gark's Story

I sat for a moment on my haunches and studied the furs. It was Rak, I was sure of it but what was he doing? The hunt was tomorrow and as one of the eldest of the young men I was expected to be up front, ahead of the younger ones with their drums and branches. In that moment, I knew what would happen if we came upon a tiger.

The moon was almost on the horizon as I made my way down into the rainforest by the river.

I had seen it many times as a child when I had come here with my mother and my grandmother- a small shrub with deep blue berries but now in the half -light it seemed to be missing. I couldn't wait much longer. I needed to be ready with the other men, as soon as it was sunrise. Why wasn't it where I'd remembered it? Had it died?

The moon was gone now and the soft blue of lightening sky told me I had no more time. In desperation, I did what I had done as a small boy and waded into the stream and began to walk up against the gentle current. And there it was, just as it had been in my childhood. Off to the left on the first rise stood the tree and as I shook it, the ripest berries fell to the ground. I gathered them up and put them in my pouch.

Before I left the river, I threw water over the fur skins and the sickly-sweet smell of animal blood hung in the air again.

In the village circle the men stood waiting and as I stepped among them Rak looked up.

'I am ready to lead the hunt'

Rak smiled broadly, as the young men looked at me approvingly. When he stepped forward I bridged the distance between us and embraced him in a solid hug- a hug that held him immoveable for a full half a minute.

The others looked on, unsure if this was a custom before the hunt that was to be observed.

Rak squirmed but I held him and tried to meet his eyes but we were too close.

When I was sure my plan had worked I pushed him away and he looked at me suspiciously.

We moved out across the grasslands and the men spread out in a phalanx, their drums and branches beating against the undergrowth.

For the first hour, we raised nothing but startled ground nesting birds and the occasional hare. By the middle of the day the sun fell upon us like a great weight, as the sweat poured into our eyes. The sticky seeds of the plains grass stuck to our skin and began to itch. The younger ones were growing restless and perhaps a little bored; disappointed that we had produced so little.

A loud 'bird cry' sounded off to the right, in the distance. One of the scouts had spotted a tiger. It was moving along the tree line shadowing a small herd of bison that were unaware of its presence. The drummers fell silent. The beaters dropped their branches and raised their spears.

As one, the hunters turned in a large sweeping curve and surrounded the end of the tree line that pointed out into the grasslands like an isthmus into a sea of green.

Rak came in from the north and I from the south. The air was still and neither the bison nor the tiger picked up our scent.

I took the berries from my pouch and crushed them into a pulp in my hands, rubbing them up my arms and face. I squeezed the acrid juice across the front of my furs and the excess ran down my thighs and dripped onto my feet.

The pungent scent filled my nostrils and my stomach began to heave.

Rak dropped down low and ran at the bison hurling his spear and seeming purposefully to miss. The bison scattered and the tiger rounded on the last straggler and turned the frightened animal in my direction. The calf dodged and weaved with the tiger close behind.

As I came into its sights, it turned and with two bounds it cleared the distance and brought me down.

The beast held my torso with its claws and the enormity of its weight. But the creature, its muzzle hard against my neck, took one deep breath and immediately released its' prey and backed away. Fleeing straight to the tree line, it began to roll in the leaf litter below a balboa tree in a desperate attempt to free itself of the smell.

Rak ran into the clearing and seeing me, moved cautiously toward my still body. His knife unsheathed, he was certain I was dead. In a moment, my own knife beside me, I would show him just how dead I was. He knelt and raised his blade. He would have to be quick before the others arrived.

A great shadow blocked out the sun and the tiger brought him down and took his throat in its jaws. Instantly I heard his neck snap like a branch underfoot. As I looked up the tiger was dragging his limp body into the undergrowth.

We killed two bison that day and the tribe ate well, till the moon disappeared ten days later. By this time, I was the new leader.

At the end of the summer we moved across the plains to seek out the tribes that lived in the mountains and the woman I had seen five moons past and who had haunted my dreams for all that time.

*There is a logic flaw in this story, that I did not explain- did you see it? I LEFT IT THERE ON PURPOSE.

It is to do with hunting, to do with what they are hunting. Think about it and then go to - Appendix- **Gark's Story Logic Flaw**

CONFLICT AND THE EMOTIONAL CORE –A SYMBIOTIC RELATIONSHIP

These two aspects of writing are central to each other

Conflict is often physical and centres on opposing forces. But Conflict is also part of the emotional landscape of a story. A story will have a Character Arc that involves an emotional dilemma/ emotional needs and desires as well as physical threat and danger. These two central issues Emotional Core and Conflict are inseparable in well told tales. The protagonist may face all sorts of perils but to truly involve the reader the focal character will have a deep and moving psychological and emotional journey. This may or may not be bound up within the physical danger. Just as possibly the emotional dilemma may be a hindrance to the overcoming of the physical threat. But when the emotional challenge is faced and understood then the physical conflict can be met head on.

WRITE ABOUT WHAT YOU KNOW

More than just a story about your Uncle Bernard

This is the piece of advice most often given to fledgling writers and it is of great value. But it is open to misinterpretation.

Writing about what you know does not need to be taken literally, although you might. It doesn't mean that you must set your stories in your street, town or country, peopling them with those that you know. All stories would be earthbound and provincial if that was the case.

Again, we return to Emotional Core and ask these questions – What are the profound or deeply moving moments of your life, what are the significant events and how did they make you feel? What are the moments of joy, despair, passion, shame, elation, desire, longing, anger that are deeply embedded in your life experience? Moments that took hold of you.

You are free to set your story anywhere and at any time for this advice relates to what you do with the characters. If you imbue them with emotionally rich experiences, with moments that are heartfelt and resonate, that have a fundamental truth about them then it doesn't matter where your story is set. You will be writing about what you know!

CHAPTER SEVEN
CREATING WORLDS

Setting
Creating Worlds {that characters can live in}
Exercise 15
Research

SETTING

Aspects of setting including time, place, demography

TIME

Future, past and present, day, night, seasons and weather all have impacts on your story. The coming of a winter that lasts at least ten years has a major effect on the characters and storyline of the *'Songs of Fire and Ice'* series. Stories set in the past that rely on true events require accurate historical research.

Robert Harris' *'Pompei'* is set a few days before the eruption of Mt Vesuvius. A hydraulic engineer arrives to investigate the parlous state of the city's water supply and discovers that the previous engineer is missing and things are not what they seem, both above and below the ground. Accurate research, that is era and location specific, is obviously required.

Stories set in the future also require their own elaboration. You must extrapolate from what we already know and extend it with your imagination, to create new possibilities and dilemmas. But once you have set up the parameters/rules/laws then you need to be consistent.

In *'I Robot'*, Isaac Asimov sets up a set of laws that define the interaction between robots and humans. While they confine the stories they also set up possibilities for the stories conflict base. Future stories ask writers many questions. How do we work, eat, play, interact with humankind? What do we aspire to/need/desire in a future world? What are the more positive or negative aspects of contemporary life and how do they manifest in the future? All these are aspects of the time your story is set in.

LOCATION

Hand in hand with time goes place. The geography of your setting is a crucial factor in story setting. Cities of the past, present or future need to be understood by both writer and reader. Buildings, roads, transportation, city centres, temples, markets and focal points need to be clearly delineated.

Stories that move through nature/ countryside/wilderness and in which elements of those landscapes play vital parts in the story also need to be clearly set out from the beginning, at least for the writer. Places along a journey become plot points and turning points in your narrative. They present mood and emotion metaphors and they will provide you with dangers and challenges for your main protagonists.

DEMOGRAPHY

The social make-up of your story is an integral factor. Does the populace have a class system or a hierarchy? Every society does. This allows for positions of status and power, of authority and punishment. It creates allegiances {often shifting} and it allows for those on the way down as well as those on the way up.

A society has belief systems and social conventions. The protagonist will often question those belief systems and will seek out truths that the belief system obscures. They will become the exception to the norm. They may become the lone outsider who is at variance with the conventions and suffocating constrictions of the greater masses.

Railing against the norm and the containment it creates is a central theme of many books including

The Scarlet Letter – Nathaniel Hawthorne

1984 – George Orwell

Brave New World – Aldous Huxley

The Chrysalids – John Wyndham

So along with aspects of time and location, demography which means the society and its' social make up all have an influence on the setting. Possession of knowledge, wealth or lack of it, status and position are elements of the demography and therefore subsets of your setting.

CREATING WORLDS {THAT YOUR CHARACTERS CAN LIVE IN}

Maps/Diagrams/Blueprints

Index Cards of Time and Space

Mind Maps

DRAW A MAP/DIAGRAM /BLUEPRINT.

Decide how big your story needs to be. The topography of the landscape will allow you to plan the physical and emotional terrain your story will cross.

EXERCISE 15

Draw maps and diagrams of where your action takes place, as a birds' eye view looking down from above.

Is your story set in part in a house? What rooms, features, and furniture will you need? Is your story set in a town? How are the streets, houses, parks, factories, roads, bridges, rivers and hills set out? Does your story involve a physical journey? Over what kind of land, sea, air or river will you travel?

Nothing that you create here is locked in. You are always free to change things as your story develops. Better ideas will always replace weaker ones.

'Wind in the Willows' and *'Lord of the Rings'* have maps and diagrams to help the reader to follow the story but you can be sure they existed when the author was writing the tale to help him. Though there is no map provided Samuel Clemens knew the Mississippi as a boy and a man and as

Mark Twain uses that geographic knowledge throughout 'The Adventures of Huckleberry Finn'.

Laying out your story in visuals terms is a great aid to structure, complications, rhythm and pace and many other writing aspects that will become apparent to you as you proceed. You need to arrive at different parts of the story as you arrive at different places. These places will be the sites of events/threats/discoveries/revelations/understandings in your story. Seeing structure in a visual diagram allows you to create a story that satisfies an audience and makes life easier for you to create.

PLACE CARDS

Either on computer or as index cards the writer sets out ideas, events, twists and turns and places them in front of them. Now you will switch them about. Here we are playing with time and space; particularly time. Can we begin our story here or here? At the middle and go forwards then back, at the end and go back to the start [story told in reverse order], at the middle and go back to the start and then move forward to the end? At present this might be difficult to imagine but when you lay out these cards either physically or on a computer you will begin to see possibilities. We do this all the time when we cut and paste on a computer screen. This is the same idea on a larger scale because it is devoted to the development of a story and it can and often should be done before the story is commenced.

Stories also rarely stay in one place and as they move from place to place they move your story along. Events come and go and characters grow and change. To lay this out with place cards is not only a way of seeing the linear progression and new ways to arrange time but also a way of seeing changes in character's emotions and circumstances. All this relates to the characters movement within the setting; their physical journey but ultimately their emotional journey.

MIND MAPS

Mind maps start with a central idea or statement in a circle/square in the middle of a page and from that central circle/square branches travel out with circles/squares on their ends and connect to even smaller branches and circles/squares.

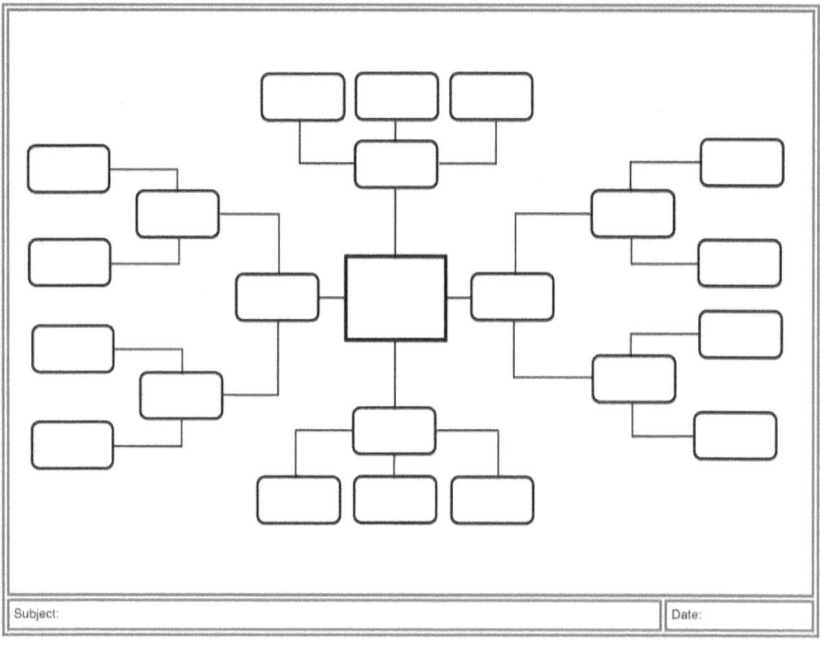

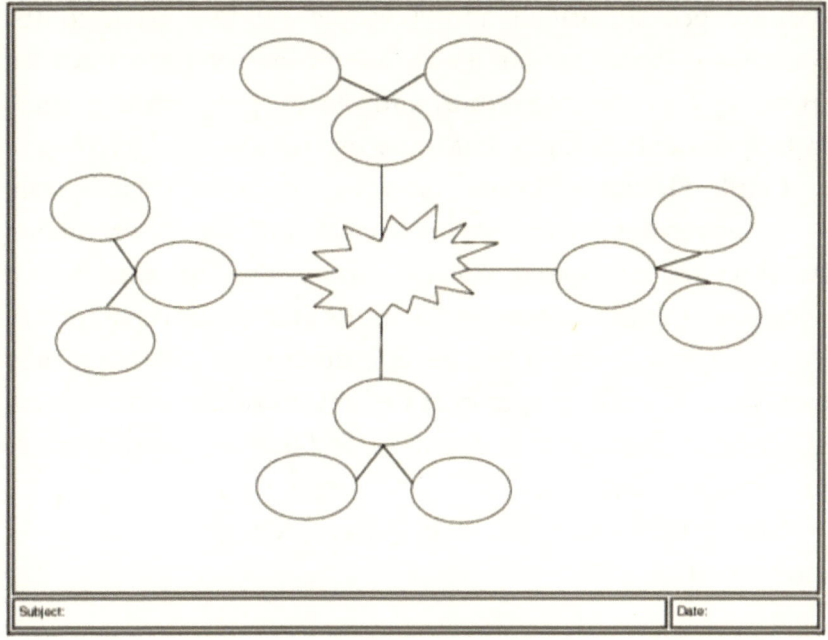

Mind maps can help create worlds or they can be used at the initial story creation point that we talked of earlier when generating story ideas.

This is a good time to talk about research

RESEARCH

There is no escaping the fact that you must do the hard yards

Research is essential to having a world that feels real for a reader.

DO NOT ASSUME IF YOU ARE CREATING AN IMAGINARY WORLD THAT YOU CONSTRUCT IT FROM YOUR HEAD, WITHOUT RESEARCH.

Whether it is a conventional world or a fantasy one you will need to research. 'Middle Earth' works because Tolkien was steeped in British and Teutonic folklore back to its' source, at least as far back as an ancient story called *'Beowulf'*. He created names and places, people and poems- in fact whole languages that draw on this knowledge.

Frank Herbert's *'Dune'* involves an entire solar system – the governments and royal houses and the desert planet Arrakis are all based on his knowledge of earthbound dynasties, middle eastern populations and desert ecosystems.

Sometimes research can be as little as how to build a billy cart, how to make ginger beer or how to ride a surfboard on a left-hand break but it could be as large as creating entire histories for civilisations.

Going that extra distance in research gives your work authenticity.

CHAPTER EIGHT
BUILDING BLOCKS

The Plotline
The Treatment
The Next Steps
First Draft and Spontaneity
Second Draft and Beyond and Forward Planning
Turning Points
The Three Act Structure Reworked
Payoffs/Twists and Riddles
Irony
Beginning at the End
Random XYZs
Exercise 16
Exercise 17
Exercise 18
Endings Yet to be Discovered
Is That It? The Climax
Plot Dump

Incluing or Foreshadowing

PLOTLINE {AND PLOT POINTS}

Plotlines and the plot points along the way

Plotting out your plot points means seeing your story in a linear way, like a timeline.

How big a story you are writing depends on how many characters and events/complications you have created

Short stories have simple settings within an easily recognisable world and peopled with only a small company of characters. These characters will have backstories, with just enough detail to explain the characters' motivation in the story.

Novels have complex settings within elaborate detailed worlds and are peopled with a larger number of characters who make decisions and enact scenarios that can be plotted along a plotline, using plot points. These characters will be deeper, richer, more complex and engaging because there is time in the pages of a novel or novella to develop them and the ramifications of what they do. They are emotionally complex, making both wise and foolish decisions and of course they will change over time [**Character Arcs**].

Plot points are the points along which your characters live. They include the day to day events [only story relevant ones please], that give your story reality but also the major moments where they change and grow or change and shrivel. They are like the stations along a railway line heading for a final terminus – the climax and resolution of your story.

A **TIMELINE** used as a **PLOTLINE** with plot points along the line.

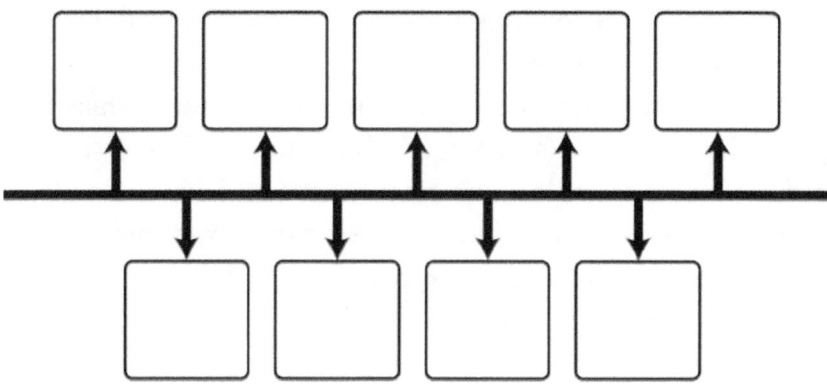

But before we go into any more detail let us make sure we understand what order things **usually** happen in, when we are in the process of creating a story.

THE TREATMENT

In which we see what is meant by a treatment and what is the treat within

Even before you come to the first draft, you should think seriously of writing out a treatment. A treatment is a version of your story without description or very much dialogue. It is a version that centres on the physical and emotional journey of your protagonist. It highlights all the plot points, turning points and climaxes.

As such it is invaluable for working out your story and character arcs and developing irony, twists and revelations. It will allow you to see flaws in your plot development. It is invaluable because of its brevity – it forces you to focus on the action and the drama both physical and emotional. It is a roadmap of where you are taking your characters and finally your readers.

Much of this will flow in a spontaneous fashion that you can tighten up, as you look back at it. It will usually flow quite fast because of its skeletal nature.

You might expect a treatment to be little more than two pages if you write a ten-page short story. If you write a hundred-page novella your treatment could be as small as twenty pages or less. A four-hundred page novel might begin with an eighty page treatment, perhaps a little less.

When you write your first draft you will beef it up with brilliant dialogue and convincing, well observed description. The treatment will be there to guide you to that devastating finish.

Of course, if you find flaws or a better way to tell the story then the treatment is the place to rejig it. Here you can move the story components around, start from a different place, change a characters' motivation, reveal a truth earlier or later. It is easier to do when you are dealing with a smaller, more manageable format. Caught in the throes of characterisation, setting and dialogue in a first draft, it is more difficult to get perspective. But even in the first draft you may rework things. To be honest reworking a story will happen throughout each and every draft. It is just easier to do major reworking in the earlier versions, especially in a treatment.

With a treatment, you can plot the rise and fall of plot points, turning points and revelations within the chapters. It allows you to see the rhythms and flow of your story arc. By placing each major change {turning point} into a chapter you can design the chapters so that they build to the chapter end. Each chapter needs to build to a revelation, a change; a surprise. The following chapter needs to explore that change and begin to build to the next turning point at that chapter's conclusion. As a reader we enjoy this process, it gives clarity and purpose to our story design.

A novel might look like this.

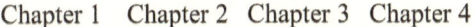

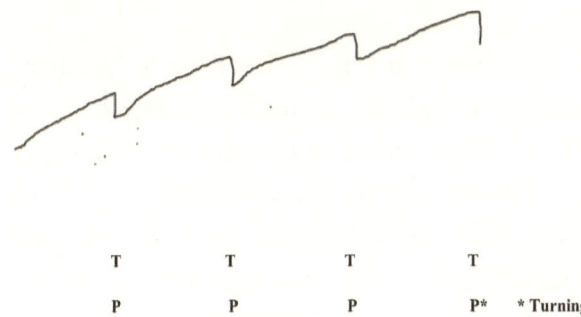

Not all stories will look like the diagram but many will have 'builds' to the end of chapters that look just like this. This is the cliff-hanger, the situation where we are left shocked, amazed, frightened, beguiled. The purpose here is to give the reader that special frisson of excitement that says' I wonder what will happen next?

THE NEXT STEPS FIRST DRAFT AND SPONTANIETY

Let us look at what happens most often in the process of creation. For natural born storytellers, the stories flow out of them. It has already flowed out in the treatment and now it is expanding into the First Draft. You put pen to paper or fingers on keyboards and the words pour out. When you are in the grip of a great story then just **'Let it Flow'**. Of course, the more you understand the fundamentals the more focused your writing will be. I hope that with all this knowledge you are still able to function naturally as a writer. You must not let all of this get in your road. All this information should exist as part of your writer's DNA.

SECOND DRAFT AND BEYOND AND FORWARD PLANNING

Having poured out all you want to tell {at least initially}, then it is time to further tweak the story structure. Lay out your plotline and then begin to look at characters, situations, arcs and all the other possibilities we have been talking about here. It is often from this Second Draft on that you will see character and situation potential, logic flaws and themes that are running through the story. Your task is to take the tools that are here and refine your story to make it the most satisfying read you can create.

LAYING OUT YOUR PLOTLINE ALLOWS YOU TO GAIN PERSPECTIVE AND TO ASK MANY QUESTIONS

When you set out index cards of plot development/story creation, as we spoke of earlier, then what we are doing is setting out a story timeline. This is the written version that gives you an overview of how your story is developing and whether it has an enough time to develop characters or situations adequately.

Most narratives move forward in a linear progression even the ones that play with time. They often rearrange linear segments in unusual configurations.

Is it constructed in a series of connected acts that allow the story to flow and for an audience to engage with the narrative?

The major plot points where events and character cause others or themselves to change are called **TURNING POINTS**. Plot points are not always turning points but turning points are always plot points.

TURNING POINTS

The points at which something dramatic happens, including a new look at the turning points of a 'classic'

These usually involve the changing of scene, the arrival of specific characters and often a change of fortune. We have all read or have had read to us the European Folktales of childhood. These books, often with illustrations, move to a new page on the turning point. Let us take a simple example that is universally known.

Our story opens at the home of Mr and Mrs Bruin of 'The Woods'. Mrs Bruin has been labouring over the cooking pot and has just ladled out three bowls of porridge for breakfast. Mr Bruin comes down the stairs followed by their young son, Baby. On discovering that their breakfast is too hot, they decide on an early morning walk in the woods, whilst it cools down. **END OF OPENING SCENE**

FIRST TURNING POINT *At this point a vagrant with no visible means of support and of no fixed address, breaks into their empty home. It is believed that she has been responsible for a series of break-ins in the area and has been fencing stolen goods to a well-known gold dealer by the name of Rumpelstiltskin, obviously an alias.*

Entering the house, she proceeds to sample and then devour some of the owners' breakfast and then to destroy their furniture.

Probably hung over from the previous night, she goes upstairs to sleep it off.

SECOND TURNING POINT *The owners arrive home to find their house wide open, their breakfast ruined or missing and the infant's chair- a priceless heirloom, handed down from bear to bear for the last hundred years, lying in pieces. Hearing snoring from the second floor, they arm themselves with a broom and Mr Bruin's Blunderbuss and begin to climb the stairs.*

THIRD TURNING POINT. *They discover the sheets of the first and second beds in a very sorry state. The hobo, having not washed for the last six months, has left the bed sheets in such a condition that they can only be taken outside and burnt. But it is the ever-observant youngster Baby, who discovers that the criminal in question is still in the house. In fact, as was reported to the police later, 'She was still in the last bed'.*

FOURTH TURNING POINT. *Realising that she was facing a term in gaol, the burglar woke from her drunken stupor and seizing the moment screamed and fled the house.*

Police have a good description of the golden haired young hoodlum and are confident of an arrest, in the near future. She is believed to be armed and dangerous and if she resists they have been ordered to 'shoot to kill!'

While I have taken a humorous approach to illustrating turning points I do not want you to think this is a trite subject. Robert McKee's wonderful book on screenwriting 'Story' describes what a turning point signifies in film but this astute observation also applies to novels. He points out that turning points create specific effects in the viewer or in our case the reader.

Surprise
Increased curiosity
Insight
New direction

He then pinpoints the scenes in certain films where these revelations and changes occur. Those same points can be found in novels.

Good writing will set up situations and character development that go against or beyond expectation. We will not see the development coming and are therefore **surprised.**

This then leads to **increased curiosity,** in which we ask of the story 'Where will this go now?' or 'What on earth does this mean?' or 'How can this be possible?' or similar questions.

From here our turning point or perhaps the next one will provide us with **insight.** Now we begin to understand where our story is headed. Now we begin to understand how our characters are operating. We begin to understand their motivation a little more.

Finally, our turning point will begin to take us in a **new direction** in which the story, at this point, leads to specific new events.

Some turning points will have only one or two of these facets – surprise, increased curiosity, insight or new direction, whilst others may have all four.

Turning points are clearly the points in a story where the

characters' lives have changed irrevocably. It is where they move into a new phase, rise or sink to another level, have revealed a vital clue, face a new danger.

THE ARRIVAL OF A TURNING POINT MEANS THE STORY MOVES IN A NEW DIRECTION OR DEVELOPS SUBSTANTIALLY.

Turning points are easy to see even in more complex stories. Most writers break up novels into chapters and each new chapter represent a minor or major turning point.

When books are condensed down into films, it is easy to see both the three act structure and the turning points that signpost each of the acts. Turning points and acts go hand in hand.

Many great stories will play with the order of the acts and the turning points. They begin at the middle or the end and go backwards and forwards. As they do they reveal character actions and choices that lead to an end that we might already know. The enjoyment is in finding out how they got there. The knowledge of where we know they will end up makes their choices all the more fascinating.

THE THREE ACT STRUCTURE REWORKED

Starting mid-story and then returning to the beginning to illuminate the ending

Earlier on we looked at the three-act structure in its simplest form. We talked about it in linear time. Our story opens, it develops complications and then it resolves. And all of this is highlighted by the Turning Points in a traditional and conventional way. Oral storytelling and myths and folktales in general relied on this orthodox form- beginning at the start and developing complications and resolutions, arriving at the end. Good authors know that there are many other ways to tell a story.

As novels became more sophisticated in the 1800's, novelists and finally screenwriters in the 20th and 21st century began to play with structure and time. Stories within stories, for instance, developed.

Now that we have some idea about Turning Points, let's look at some of the elements that can set up early in your Turning Points to make a pleasing pay off later.

Beginning closer to the climax and then returning to the start is a very powerful storytelling mode. We capture our readers with *'How did they find themselves in this predicament?'* We then go back and from the first scene, in a basically linear fashion, we build in the ironies, complications and twists toward the point that we began with, the one that we know already. Arriving at that point we are totally engaged, fully knowledgeable of all that led up to that climactic moment.

Look at one great example of this.

Many know the story of *'Frankenstein'* as the tale of an obsessed man of science Dr Victor Frankenstein, determined to defeat death, who creates a man from human remains. When it is animated by electricity, Frankenstein abandons the experiment in terror. After which, the piteous and uncomprehending creature is met with fear and hostility from all who meet him. Finally, angry and despairing the monster runs amok lashing out and seeking revenge, until he is finally defeated.

This is of course the story reduced to its lowest common denominator and designed to fit the demands of both silent and then early 'talkie' cinema, at the start of the Twentieth Century.

The novel is far deeper and asks many profound questions about science, God, life, death and responsibility. Only Kenneth Branagh's film *'Mary Shelley's Frankenstein'* comes anywhere near addressing these questions, by telling the story in the same way as the novel.

The book begins with a letter written from an ice bound ship trapped in frozen wastes, somewhere in the Arctic. As the crew watch from the deck, a man of monstrous proportions appears on the horizon, driving a dog sled at a relentless pace.

Soon after another man is discovered on the ice and brought on board. He is Victor Frankenstein, who after wandering in and out of delirium for several days, finally recovers enough to tell his tale to the ship's captain. A story of how he came to be there and the identity of the monstrous man the crew saw in the distance.

We then go back to his youth and his first and only love, his days at university, his growing obsession with death and resurrection and the creation of his great folly and nemesis.

We follow both his narrative and that of the creature, who we both revile and sympathise with. Finally, the climax of the book and the film is played out tragically, on the arctic ice between the creator and his creation.

Many other novels of the 19th century commence in similar ways. 20th and 21st century novels and films use this structure constantly. To begin other than at the start requires the audience to ask questions of the main characters and their predicament.

Who are these characters and what is there relationship to

one another?

What had the protagonist done to find themselves in this position?

Is the main character's motivation understandable?

Are situations really as they appear on the surface?

Are there characters in the story, as it opens, that are perhaps not what they appear to be?

Good authors know that a story, which tantalizes with a powerful predicament and puzzling characters, deserves a structure that plays with time and sequence.

PAY OFFS/TWISTS AND RIDDLES

Looking at surprising your audience and a man pays the ultimate price

Authors surprise their audience. One of the most satisfying things they can do is to create revelations and climaxes.

You have already set up puzzles, mysteries and expectations. Now, usually in the late Complication [Act Two] or early in the Resolution [Act Three] the truths are revealed. Sometimes they will confirm what went before but other times they will surprise or shock the reader. But no matter how much they shock, they must be believable. You must be able to say, *"Yes, I am surprised but I can see how we arrived at that. It makes logical and emotional sense."*

Spoiler Alert At this point read Charles Dickens', *'A Tale of Two Cities'* or if time is an issue watch the film version but do not read on till you have done this. {Appendix Recommendation lists.}

In *'A Tale of Two Cities'* the antihero of our story takes the place of a man that is condemned to death. In the morning, he will face an angry mob and the guillotine.

Why does he do this? How can he possibly get away with this deceit?

We know that he has been a drunkard and a waster all his life. He loves Lucie, a married woman and adores her daughter, to whom he has become a favourite uncle. And for them he would do anything to keep them safe.

We have also seen, in Act One, in the set- up, that he bears a striking resemblance to Lucie's husband.

In our final scene, as fantastic and unpredictable as it is, he takes the other man's place at the execution. No-one among the guards or the crowd recognises the switch. Everyone sees what they expect to see. Only one prisoner, a young seamstress girl, realizes that he is an imposter. And to her he explains why.

This is one of the great twists and most fabulous if heartbreaking pay-offs in literature. Perhaps one day you will create a character with the same level of tragic nobility, in one of your stories.

J.K. Rowling achieved the same with the death and later revelations about Severus Snape. {**SEE CHARACTER ARC CHAPTER FIVE**}

Twists and pay offs are surprising and pleasing but when they are IRONIC they have a power that goes way beyond being just unexpected.

IRONY

We look at the 'Ironic Twist' {and other dance crazes}. How fate steps in and gives us exactly what we didn't want

Dictionary definition: **Irony-Incongruity between what might be expected and what occurs. In literature irony is set up for humorous, dramatic or rhetorical purposes.**

Irony is one of the most powerful tools at a writer's disposal. Previously I described some of the twists in *'A Tale of Two Cities'* but they are more than mere twists in plot development. They are made the more profound because they are the actions and plans of characters that turn against the protagonists.

In 1757 a young Dr Mannette is called to the Evremonde estate and there discovers a young man dying of sword wounds and a young woman who has been violated by the master of the house. He decides to report these transgressions to the authorities but before he can he is arrested and locked in prison- The Bastille, for the next eighteen years.

The perpetrator of these crimes the Marquis St Evremonde, a cruel and wilful member of the aristocracy, is murdered by one of the peasant revolutionaries – the father of a boy he had run over in his carriage.

Finally freed in 1775, the Doctor is nursed in the home of poor wine sellers -the DeFarges'. It is above the wine shop that Dr Manette is reunited with his daughter Lucy who is now a young woman of twenty.

Charles Darnay, a Frenchman working and living in Britain, returns to his new home in England across the channel. He had been a member of an aristocratic family but, ashamed of what his family had done to the poor, had changed his name and gone to England to earn an honest living. During the trip, he befriends Dr Manette, Lucy Manette and her companion Miss Pross. On arrival in Britain he is arrested and falsely charged with aiding the French [Britain's enemy at the time].

Accused by a petty criminal he is defended by Sydney Carton. Carton, whilst a brilliant lawyer, has spent most of his adult life as a drunkard. Darnay's case is won on the strength of one point - that the identification of the accused might be in question. Carton points out that many men look similar in the half light. That he himself bears a strong resemblance to Darnay. The jury are convinced and Charles is acquitted.

Now freed Charles Darnay, in the company of Lucie Manette, thanks Sydney Carton for his efforts. Sydney Carton becomes a family friend and the years pass by. Charles and Lucie have married and have a daughter 'Little Lucie'. Sydney is the child's favourite uncle and he dotes on her, though secretly he loves her mother and has since the first moment he met her.

In 1789 the French Revolution begins and an angry mob storm the Bastille, among them is Monsieur DeFarge, who goes to the cell that was once occupied by Dr Manette. Here he finds hidden in a crack between two stones a bundle of papers.

THESE INTERCONNECTED CHARACTERS HAVE PASTS THAT CROSS EACH OTHER. IT IS NOW THAT **THE IRONY BEGINS.**

'The Reign of Terror' commences and both the guilty and the innocent are tried and executed.

Charles Darnay returns to France to defend his now imprisoned servant, who stayed in France to look after his estate. Charles is arrested as he enters Paris as a member of the Evremonde family and an emigrant.

Lucie, Dr Manette, Little Lucie, Miss Pross and Sydney Carton rush to Paris to save him. There Dr Manette wins his freedom by appealing to the mob claiming that he is a friend of the Revolution and has suffered like them under the aristocracy.

But Darnay is soon arrested again and this time he is denounced by Madame DeFarge. She is the sister of the boy and the girl who died at the hands of the Evremondes. This time not even Dr Manette can save him. When Madame DeFarge reads out Dr Manette's letter, written from The Bastille, it seals Darnay's fate. For within that letter, in the pits of despair at his imprisonment, Dr Manette denounces the Evremondes –'Them and their descendants to the last of their race'.

Now Charles will die within twenty four hours. That night, delighted with the result, Madame DeFarge boasts that the daughter and the child will follow him to their deaths also. She goes to where the Manettes are staying but is met by the formidable Miss Pross and dies by her own hand when her gun discharges.

Sydney Carton realises that he alone can save the situation. He visits Darnay in his cell that night and tricks him into *changing clothes with him. He then overpowers Darnay and gets his accomplice to take the half-conscious man out. He stays behind and goes to the guillotine knowing that he has saved an entire family from destruction and that they will always remember him in their hearts.*

Let us look at the 'What Ifs' that the author would have used within the creation of this story, for these provide a key to the irony.

What if you denounce a whole family for their crimes but decades later one of them falls in love with your daughter? And now your written testimony will be the document that damns your son in law?

What if your resemblance to another man saves his life once? What if you know that it could work again but this time you will need to die in his place?

What if the dissolute life you have lived can finally be redeemed but can only be so if you pay with your life?

What if the love and respect that you have craved, especially from the woman you have loved from afar, will finally be realized? It will be realized because you will have died to save her family. They will name their first boy after you and he will live to be all you had hoped for yourself.

Clearly irony is a powerful tool in the hands of great writers creating unforeseen twists and providing stories with real jeopardy.

BEGINNING AT THE END

At the most desperate moment he woke up to find it was only a dream. Why knowing the climax is vital. Introducing

XYZs.

We all know that moment as a child, when we wrote or had another child's story read to us and it ended with 'but then she awoke and found that it was only a dream'. Why do some stories end like this? As wonderful as some of our ideas are they are not always complete stories.

People have come to me saying, *'I have this great idea for a story!'* And my reply after hearing the setup is *'How does it end?'* And yes, you guessed it, they don't have an ending. They were hoping I might supply one. But it's not my story to begin with and finding that elusive ending will take some workshopping.

Finding satisfactory endings that really work is the ultimate writer's challenge. So why not start from the ending? Here are some endings I call.......

X Y ZS

The reverse of What Ifs

They are endings looking for a beginning -the reverse of **'WHAT IFs'**. Let's begin with a well-known ending from Shakespeare. Try to put together the threads of the story that led up to this ending. Perhaps you already know the story, if not try to piece together the events before this climax.

XYZ 1. HAMLET

Prince Hamlet faces off against his sworn enemy Laertes in a sword fight. Hamlet's uncle the King, the Queen and the court look on. The King and Laertes are determined that Hamlet must die and the previous night set their venomous traps. The

King aware that Hamlet knows of his crime is determined to have him dead, determined to hide that secret from the world.

Laertes' sword is tipped in poison and Hamlet's goblet of wine is laced with the same. Hamlet is cut with the sword but during the fight the swords are accidentally exchanged. In between rounds the Queen drinks to Hamlet's victory from his cup. The King begs her not to but it is too late. The poisoned sword now in Hamlet's hands wounds Laertes. The Queen staggers and falls. Laertes doubles over but in his death throes tells Hamlet that the King's to blame.

Enraged Hamlet stabs the King and then pours the rest of the wine down the King's throat. Hamlet staggers to his friend Horatio and dies in his arms.

   Why is Laertes the sworn enemy of Hamlet ?
      Why is the King determined to have Hamlet dead?
      What is the King's secret that must die with Hamlet?
      With such a spectacular ending what went before?
      This is the lead up to that ending

Hamlet, Prince of Denmark, is visited on the battlements of the castle, by the ghost of his father. The ghost calls on Hamlet to avenge his murder. A murder committed by the dead King's brother Claudius. Claudius now has taken the throne and married his widow Gertrude, Hamlet's mother. Hamlet is unsure what to do next and pretends madness. He hires actors to present a play about a man who kills his brother to become king. He watches Claudius' reaction. Claudius runs from the play in terror and Hamlet is convinced of his guilt. He goes to his mother to plead with her to leave Claudius. Someone is hiding behind a tapestry listening to what is being said. Hamlet stabs the tapestry believing it is the King. Instead it is old Polonius a minister of the court. He is also the father of Hamlet's consort Ophelia. She loses her mind when she hears what has happened and mad with grief throws herself into the river and drowns. Her brother Laertes returns to court bent on revenge for his father and sister's death. King Claudius plots with Laertes to poison Hamlet.

XYZ 2. Here is another ending.

EXERCISE 16

Create a story that leads up to this?

Alessandro looked out from the cabin of the 'Mediterranean Wind', a fourteen- tonne trawler out of the Bay of Biscay. It was two hours before the daylight would finally be gone but he had enough time to investigate what lay off to the starboard side, just up ahead.

From here it looked like a schooner and from its' position apparently in trouble.

Two minutes later his observation proved true. A thirty-five foot ketch with a broken mast leant forty five degrees to port. It had taken in a great deal of water and was at least two thirds below the surface of a becalmed sea. He made to on the upright side and stepped across walking the rim of the Plimsoll line which because of the lean now served as the deck.

A man, dressed in a torn Tee and a pair of cut off jean shorts, lay dead and slumped toward the water, tied to the main mast and covered in dried salt spray. He had been that way for some time and his body had stiffened.

Just then the water and all that lay below deck shifted dramatically and the prow rose up, as the stern began to slide plumb-like towards the ocean floor. Allesandro grabbed the side railing as the forward hatch sprang open.

'You better get off! She go down pretty quick!' offered Miguel his first mate from the safety of the trawler.

'Just wanna look below! '

Hand over hand he pulled himself up the deck to the broken hatch cover.

Below deck, the world floated in seawater. Pillows, mattresses, cans of tinned food, a waterproof torch its' light on, bobbing in the foam and dancing light across the inner hull.

And there pressed into the far corner, floating face down lay two bodies – a man and a woman.

The ketch heaved again and threw Allessandro over the side.

Moments after he was back on board the 'MW' and towelling dry. They pulled away and watched from a distance, taking note of its registration and its name- 'The Promise'.

Ten minutes later there was nothing on the surface to show what had once been there. Nothing except one red high heel shoe floating on a dark blue ocean that stretched on forever.

What went before this story? Your challenge is to look at what is in the story, all the elements and create the events that led up to this ending.

RANDOM XYZS

Like our 'What Ifs' these are story starters that begin at the end and ask you to create what went before.

EXERCISE 17

The rifleman and Horace find a way out of their troubled lives but you must tell us what went before

He put down the rifle and walked away. He knew now that he would have no more need for it. She was standing across the river. He pushed the boat into the middle of the stream and stroked towards her. Behind him on the disappearing shore lay the body. The one that had haunted and troubled him all his life, now lay still. In a few hours, the rising tide would sweep it downstream to the sea.

In the darkness, Horace caught the number nine bus and walked upstairs. He sat down and held the briefcase to his chest. After all the misunderstandings and the accusations, he would now be able to prove his innocence. Would he be able to go back to his old life? He doubted it but somehow this was not such a sad moment. No, not at all! He looked out over Primrose Park where the first joggers were beginning their early morning ordeals. The sun was coming up and for once in his life Horace did not dread the coming day.

Write story synopses that explain how each of these characters arrived here.

EXERCISE 18

Write five more endings and see if they lead you to the stories that went before.

ENDINGS YET TO BE DISCOVERED

Many writers do not know how their story will end. Instead they set up all the mechanics of Act I and Act II including setting, characters, backstory, motivation, quest, turning points and then, as they write the scenes, the ending reveals itself to them. Some writers will write no other way, as they want to be surprised by how the story evolves and they would lose interest if they knew for certain how it would end right from the start. There are many ways to plan and to write a book.

IS THAT IT? THE CLIMAX

Is the climax satisfying or otherwise? Including the sin of Deus et Machina

As we approach the end of a story we reach its' climax and this must satisfy an audience. If you set up a formidable menace or villain that consumes the town, takes one by one the lesser lieutenants until it reaches the main protagonist then your defeat of that threat needs to be in proportion to the villain/creature's danger and devastation. You cannot have them defeated in relative ease.

If you create a great yearning within your main character so that they have struggled to attain some goal, personal or societal, psychological, physical, emotional or spiritual than the moment of attainment must be significant. They must pay a price and have earned this exulted position. If they have, then the audience will be satisfied.

Deus et Machina

Audiences take a dim view of this too. A Deus et Machina means an act of God – a convenient way to kill off your danger with a simple but ultimately unsatisfying intervention of God or Fate. The most well-known of these is probably H.G. Wells' ending to the *'War of the Worlds'*.

Unable to defeat the Martian invasion, with conventional weapons, the populace is in full retreat. After months of annihilating defeats, they are astonished to discover that the Martian war machines have ground to a halt. Inside the pods they find the aliens slumped at the controls, the victims of germs, as harmless as the common cold but fatal to them. This ending was satisfactory back in the early twentieth century but now such a pat and wimpy ending would be, I believe, unacceptable.

You need to have your protagonist pay dearly – great effort, great pain and near defeat need to be part of the confrontation leading up to the climax.

PLOT DUMP

Coming to the end then revealing all that you were not told is a cheat

This is one of the sins of writing that discerning readers will not forgive you for. At its' worst, it comes at the climax and is a series of facts and bits of information that explain how we arrived at our conclusion, e.g. *'And that's why I know you are the infamous cat burglar!'* {after copious amounts of fact revelations}. All of which have **not** been apparent during the narrative itself.

Other times 'plot dumping' is just another way of saying exposition, e.g.' *As you know Jonathan we are here to explore the .....* [add boring, lazy writing here]'

This kind of writing is always a sign of poor design in your story structure. Information needs to be embedded in the story and appear seamlessly in conversation, found objects, places, texts within the tale, character revelations and to a lesser degree thought processes.

INCLUING OR FORESHADOWING

What clues to include so that readers conclude with a conclusion, at the story's conclusion. Clear?

Some writers know this as foreshadowing. Incluing is what a good writer does. All or almost all the vital information for us to draw conclusions from are gradually and strategically placed into spots in the tale and unfold effortlessly in your superbly controlled narrative. The clues to the denouement are everywhere but subtly positioned to not draw too much attention to themselves. This has also been called telegraphing but that is a term from another century relating to a means of communication long gone.

CHAPTER NINE
ADDING SUBSTANCE

Creating Detail
Exercise 19
Creating Atmosphere/Mood
Exercise 20
Exercise 21
Thematic Foreshadowing
Pace and Rhythm
Emotional States
Exercise 22
Writing Place and Action
Exercise 23
Metaphors and Similes
Exercise 24
Landscape as Metaphor
Exercise 25

CREATING DETAIL

The Game of Continue/Expand/Continue

This is a drama game to illustrate how storytelling and story writing are similar and how each is a balancing act between action and description.

In the game of Continue/Expand/Continue two people sit cross legged facing each other. One is the storyteller and the other is the story controller. The storyteller begins their tale and the controller will use the commands 'expand 'and 'continue' to direct and reveal the story. The story can be real or imagined, that is immaterial. It is the technique and its' results that are important.

STORYTELLER

Last week, something very strange happened to my family and me. We had just left the local shopping mall when we were followed by a large black car.

STORY CONTROLLER

Expand on car.

STORYTELLER

It was a big, black car with a noisy engine and a silver grill on the front. The windows were tinted dark blue and you couldn't see inside.

STORY CONTROLLER

Continue.

STORYTELLER

The car stayed two car lengths behind us for several blocks. It slowed when we slowed and sped up when we did. Until we came to a railway crossing....

STORY CONTROLLER

Expand on railway crossing.

STORYTELLER

The crossing cut the main road in half and two large red and white barriers came down a full minute before the train would appear. Cars four deep, on either side of the barriers, came to a halt. People dashed across, looking tentatively up the track for the hundred tons of silver grey steel that was approaching and whose sound preceded it, like a dragon's roar.

The storyteller proceeds with the action but the demands of the story controller force them to describe and to create detail before returning to the action again.

EXERCISE 19

Try the game with a partner. It will give you a good feel for description and then try it as a written exercise. It is the balancing act that you do as a writer that holds your readers' interest. Your story should move at an appropriate pace and at certain junctures it will create descriptive images that flesh out your setting.

In a nutshell- action is for character.
-description/atmosphere is for setting.

Although there will be some overlap, in which characters are described and settings have some action within themselves e.g. The Sea.

Now that we have a developing idea of how action and description relate to one another, let's look at how to create atmosphere within a scene.

CREATING ATMOSPHERE/MOOD

Three or Four senses good/Five senses bad [Maybe]

What creates atmosphere? How do you capture the essence of a place? A reading experience creates mental images and sense memories. As a reader, we convert words into pictures but just as easily we call on other sense memories-taste, smell, sound and touch to flesh out those pictures.

Once again this is a question of balance – you can activate a scene and may make it clumsy if you use all five sense descriptions, in a single paragraph. There is a hierarchy of the senses – obviously sight, sound and smell are the predominant senses to describe and set atmosphere. These are the first senses to activate when we arrive in a new place. Next comes touch then taste.

Feel {Touch} can relate to the temperature or weather conditions i.e. Wind on face, cold clamminess, fog against skin. [Feel is about the effect on skin and is not an emotional state]

Taste is used the least of all and if you have thrown it in, to use up all the senses, then don't- THIS IS OVERKILL. Taste does not come up very often and should be very specific when used.

RULE- Use the first three senses SIGHT, SOUND, SMELL and add the fourth TOUCH where appropriate and don't labour the final one TASTE.

EXERCISE 20

Sample Descriptive Paragraph about Place
Go through this paragraph and identify which senses are being used in these sentences. Notice that this is an example that does use senses but does not deal with emotions or thoughts, to any great degree.

The street was humid; the continuous hum of languages and accents hung in the air with the sweat. A faulty neon sign flashed in the puddles left after the early evening downpour. Yellow- green- blackness, yellow- green- blackness in time with the electric buzz of its wiring. Ozone scent mixed with stir-fry and boiling noodles wafting out of every open doorway. The 'Thuk Thuk', of distant rotors approaching, told him that time was short.

He thought he could hide among the milling crowds in Chinatown but he realized, as an Anglo, he was more recognizable here than anywhere else. Now the broad sweep of the searchlight danced; crisscrossing the sea of Asian faces like some giant paint stroke, daubing each body momentarily in a splash of white.

At the end of the street stood the pier, its dips of assorted party lights disappearing into the distance; into the total blackness of sky and sea beyond. Here possibly was safety! If the tide was out, the solid towering pylons below the boardwalk would offer sanctuary, if only till the first light of morning.

Take note of what senses appear first, second, third etc.
Does the order in which the senses are revealed seem logical?
Which senses appear the most?
Why do you think that is?

EXERCISE 21

Write a description, of a place or an activity or even a character that relies on the senses, to illustrate it to the reader. You may use some emotional reactions and mental perceptions but keep them to a minimum, make it as much as possible, a 'Sense Description Exercise'.

THEMATIC FORESHADOWING

Subtle intimations leading to climaxes in Story Design

One of the most pleasing and effective tropes writers employ is to create suggestions within the story that hint at what will come later, either psychologically [**Emotional Core**] or physically [**Conflict**] or both.

Objects, places, snatches of conservation, brief meetings, hand written notes, photos, paintings, clothing- really almost anything can serve as a signpost of what will happen later as a payoff. *'Rebecca'* by Daphne du Maurier offers many instances of this technique. The tale of a shy, ineffectual young woman who marries an older man and becomes the mistress of a large manor house [Manderley] in rural England. She has replaced the previous wife Rebecca, who drowned in mysterious circumstances a year earlier.

Intimidated by the head of the household and the roles she must undertake she feels totally inadequate- the house and grounds seem to be conspiring against her. Clothes, rooms, paintings, gardens, pets, buildings and landscape all remind her of her gaucheness and inexperience. The entire house is imbued with the presence of the late Rebecca de Winter*, the seemingly perfect wife and hostess whose memory and spirit reaches out of the grave to destroy the young woman's prospects.

Even something as innocuous as the daily menus becomes a metaphor for the power struggle between the draconian, domineering head of house Mrs Danvers and our heroine. Signatures, handwriting and notes are all powerful motifs that carry accusation, intimidation, dread and finally liberation.

The entire novel is a study in minutiae, not only highlighting her fears and inadequacies but the lies and mysteries that are Manderley – a house full of deceit, betrayal and murder.

Du Maurier uses these signposts and motifs to create an enclosed universe that drives the main character towards an inevitable conclusion.

This technique is especially effective for creating dark and mysterious texts.

PACE AND RHYTHM

How words create rhythm and the length of sentences create pace. Identifying pace and rhythm specific to the point in a plot

Simply put, pace is the speed at which the words and sentences are naturally read. This gives us a feel for the action and the tension. Rhythm is the rise and fall of the words, the

---

* Notice again, the use of a very specific Character Name *'de Winter'* to denote the coldness of both the character and the setting.

sound and sound patterns formed by the words, whether they are read aloud or inside your head.

PACE

Think of pace as the way in which you might walk your neighbourhood street

You walk leisurely and this gives you time to take in the sights, sounds and smells. The early summer morning embraces you, as the smell of barbeques drift in and the droning bees move lazily from red Bougainvillea to white - yellow Frangipani.

Then, out from behind a gate you are ambushed by a small, vicious dog. You are moving swiftly, trying to avoid the mongrel snapping at your heels. You shout, kick out but the snarling predator is on all sides at once.

Writing can be like this. You are taking the time to create atmosphere, to place your reader in the protagonist's mindset, to create a feeling of anticipation or dread or whatever.... Your sentences will stretch out, full of descriptive words and images, sensory mind pictures and sense memories.

Then you are threatened, challenged, the clock is ticking, you are fearful, exhilarated, confused, a myriad of different possibilities. When these emotions and situations take over a narrative the descriptive phrases tend to become sharply focused. The pace quickens. The sentences become shorter, delivered in a clipped manner. Often, they involve only sight and sound.

Look at these two passages and notice the difference in pace, imagery, senses and sentence length.

It was a bright cold day in April, and the clocks were striking thirteen. Winston Smith, his chin nuzzled into his breast in an effort to escape the vile wind, slipped quickly through the glass doors of Victory Mansions, though not quickly enough to prevent a swirl of gritty dust from entering along with him.

The hallway smelt of boiled cabbage and old rag mats. At one end of it a coloured poster, too large for indoor display, had been tacked to the wall. It depicted simply an enormous face, more than a metre wide: the face of a man of about forty-five, with a heavy black moustache and ruggedly handsome features. Winston made for the stairs. It was no use trying the lift. Even at the best of times it was seldom working, and at present the electric current was cut off during daylight hours. It was part of the economy drive in preparation for Hate Week. The flat was seven flights up, and Winston, who was thirty-nine and had a varicose ulcer above his right ankle, went slowly, resting several times on the way. On each landing, opposite the lift-shaft, the poster with the enormous face gazed from the wall. It was one of those pictures which are so contrived that the eyes follow you about when you move. BIG BROTHER IS WATCHING YOU, the caption beneath it ran.

Opening paragraph of '1984' by George Orwell

The pace here is measured with time enough to take in all the sights, sounds and smells. However, in this passage…

Snape said nothing, but walked forwards and pushed Malfoy roughly out of the way. The three Death Eaters fell back without a word. Even the werewolf seemed cowed.

Snape gazed for a moment at Dumbledore, and there was revulsion and hatred etched in the harsh lines of his face.

Severus..please...

Snape raised his wand and pointed directly at Dumbledore.

AVADA KEDAVRA!

A jet of green light shot from the end of Snape's wand and hit Dumbledore squarely in the chest.

Final paragraph of the chapter *'The Lightning Struck Tower'*- *'Harry Potter and the Half-Blood Prince'* by J.K. Rowling

The writing here is short and sharp. The sentences are not top heavy with description because they are devoted to action. This also is pace and rhythm serving the intent of the story.

RHYTHM

Rhythm is something that comes naturally. It is the way you use both words and sentences, it is as the name implies, a kind of music of words. It has timing and meter and creates a flow in the language. It should have a rise and fall that serves the narrative, at that moment in the story. Like all natural gifts it is improved upon by constant practise.

Look at a page of writing you have enjoyed. Try to pick up the rhythm. What is it that the author has done? You can easily see it in lines of poetry and song lyrics. But it is also there on a page of prose {it needs to be unpacked a little more}.

Here is an extract from Tim Winton's *'Breath'* that gives you a feel for his word rhythm.

'One November afternoon I coasted down to the river on my bike to have a jump off the plank but when I got there four girls and somebody's mother were slithering up and down the bank, yanking at their ears and screaming that there was a boy in the water, that he was drowning right beneath them. Naturally they didn't know which boy because they were from out of town, but they knew he was a boy for he'd been there a minute ago and simply hadn't come up from a dive and there were sharks and couldn't I for God's sake stop asking questions and just get on with doing something....................'

Notice the pace of this story. Firstly, it is a second-hand story told to us as an anecdote and it has little sense of urgency. The pace is not like that of the 'Harry Potter' excerpt and the rhythm of the writing adds to the laconic feel. Listen to the rhythm and feel it in the writing. This is an author taking his time to tell this story.

One November afternoon/ I coasted down to the river on my bike/

To have a jump off the plank/

But when I got there/ four girls and somebody's mother were/

Slithering up and down the bank/

Yanking at their own ears/

And screaming that there was a boy in the water/

That he was drowning right beneath them.

There is a set up here that is relatively measured. However, it should then develop a quick staccato rhythm, a sense of urgency since we are talking about a drowning and the action required to save the boy. Look what happens next.

'Sun blazed down in rods through the big old gums. There were dragonflies in the air above us. I saw a towel near the diving plank and beside it a grubby pair of thongs, so I had no reason to doubt there was a crisis. Only the sluggish water seemed harmless and these females, who were making a frightful noise, looked so strangely out of place. I should have twigged.'

This is even more relaxed. He is already giving us clues to not be dragged in to the situation. Sunlight, dragonflies, grubby thongs, harmless sluggish water, these females and finally *'I should have twigged.'*

Have you got it yet? The pace, the rhythm, the images and descriptions are all leading away from the urgency of what writing about drowning should look like.

'But I went into action on their behalf. As I bolted out to the sagging end of the springboard the wood was hot and familiar underfoot. I looked down at the wind ruffled surface and tried to think. I decided that it would be best to wade in from the bank, to work my way out by feel, and just keep diving and groping in the hope of touching something human. There wasn't time to go looking for help. I was it.'

Our pace has quickened and rhythm has changed but still not to the degree expected of saving a drowning boy. But we are being led into the urgency of the situation. There are strong deliberate words such as 'bolted', 'diving and groping' and of course the final sentences – *'There wasn't time to go looking for help. I was it.'*

But this change of pace is a set up.

'I felt myself rise to the moment- put-upon but taller all of a sudden- and before I could embark upon my mission, or even pull my shirt off, Ivan Loon burst from the water. He came up so close to shore with such a feral shriek the woman fell back on the mud as if shot. ....Loonie started to laugh.'

This has all been a practical joke and the rhythm and the pace have kept us a little distanced from the events, so that we are fooled but not as much as the woman. Here is an example of where the pace and rhythm are different to what they might be if this drowning was not a put on but was instead desperately real.†

Rhythm is a musical form and, even if you are not a musician, you have natural rhythm occurring within you. You have a steady heartbeat, the rise and fall of your breath, these are natural metronomes.

Do not be put off; even if you cannot keep time with music, writing moves at a slow enough pace that you can control your writing's rhythm. You are composing here for others, that is the narrator and the reader.

It is difficult to teach rhythm but it helps if you can recognise it. Become familiar with it in writer's work, hear it

---

† Note the appropriateness of using 'Loon' as the name of the trickster. [see **CHARACTER NAMES**]

in what you read. The more you recognise it, the more you will be able to apply it, to your own writing. With practise, you will be able to create your own rhythms, alternating them to serve pace and narrative.

Best of all you will be able to return to your own writing and rework phrases, paragraphs and pages to make them flow with the appropriate rhythm and pace.

EMOTIONAL STATES

Using description of body language to convey characters' emotions

Often what characters are feeling is conveyed by simply telling the reader what they felt. For example, 'Charlie felt unease as he opened the cellar door'. Try not to describe how a character is feeling too often. Use it minimally and it will have far greater effect.

To describe instead – hair standing on end, clamminess in the palm of her hands, beads of perspiration on his forehead is far more powerful.

She ground her teeth.

He broke into a smile.

He balled his fists and held them straight against his sides.

Charlie's muscles tightened as he opened the cellar door.

These are all examples that, through descriptions of body language, allow the reader to feel the characters' elation, anxiety, concern, fear etc. The reader fills in the gaps. They do the work and of course, they feel far more involved in the narrative. This is much better than 'Philip felt troubled', 'Maddie felt pleased'. But to be this kind of effective writer you will need to become adept at reading 'body language' and turning it into prose.

CARDINAL RULE- THE WRITER USES BODY LANGUAGE DESCRIPTORS THEN LETS THE READER FILL IN THE EMOTIONAL GAPS.

EXERCISE 22

Create a number of phrases that capture the emotional state of these characters using body language to describe emotional states.

Example: Saul his jaw clenched, barked his orders, {ANGER/RESOLVE}

Philip ..... {FEAR}
Celia ......{EMFATUATION}
Marie......{ FRUSTRATION}
Andre......{CURIOSITY}
Morgan.....{SORROW}

WRITING PLACE AND ACTION

We travel from A to B, from entrance to object[ive] writing passages that create setting and action

Here is an exercise that allows you to concentrate on action and place; leaving out emotional and psychological subtext. It is done with a partner.

Together or separately write a passage that goes from point A –the start of the scene to point B – the object or objective [physical or psychological] of the scene. Be descriptive enough in the telling of the scene that the other person is able to follow the reading- as a kind of set of instructions that they act out. A narrated mime.

Here is an example.

The gravel drive announced his arrival far too loudly. The grass was a safer bet. From there he moved silently across the lawn until he was at eyelevel with the ground floor window. There was no movement inside the house.

In the driveway, he put his hand on the car's bonnet. Still warm; they had arrived only minutes ago. She could be upstairs or perhaps down in the basement.

Behind the foliage was a square of louvered slats. Flattening himself out on the ground he grabbed one of the slats. They held with years of stiff resistance and then as one, gave way with a much too loud squeal. From his prone position, he could see a large concrete space below. Empty: she had to be upstairs. He pulled the window covering away and slid in, clutching the sill and dangling his body into the open space. The concrete cavern boomed as he hit the ground and once again unwillingly announced his presence.

From there a quick dash up the stairs in the half light and a turn of the handle brought him to the foyer and silence.

He climbed the sweeping staircase in twos until he stood on the first floor landing. Opening the first door on the right, there she stood. Not bound, not gagged but coolly holding a champagne flute and casually looking out the window. 'Ah, the cavalry has arrived!' she smirked.

Picture this as a narration that is acted out across a performance space?

If the written words can be acted out then we are able to create pictures in the mind of a reader. Here the thrust of the writing is about action and suspense so the writing stays with what is being physically done – nothing about emotional subtext and very little in the way of atmospheric writing. **What is achieved is a small cinematic moment in the reader's mind.**

* There are moments in this narrative where it was possible to humanize the character by putting the reader inside his head but this was not done since the exercise is about action, about setting and movement. Ideally you would briefly get inside his thoughts to draw the reader in. At the moment, that passage is one step removed, in a third person observer mode only. A balance between internal thought and physical action is needed if this is a passage from an actual story rather than a specific kind of exercise.

GOOD WRITERS KNOW WHEN TO SHIFT FROM EMOTIONAL SUBTEXT/INTERNAL THOUGHT PROCESSES TO ATMOSPHERE TO ACTION WRITING. THEY ARE ALWAYS IN CONTROL OF WHAT THEY WRITE.

EXERCISE 23

Write a piece that is principally place and movement and have your partner act it out.

The words should create a sense of where you are and what you are doing. Be aware of pace and rhythm. Keep the passage to sound and visuals only, as in the example. Create a number of these kinds of passages.

You could be:

Running for a train in a subway tunnel.
Browsing in the department store and aware that you are being watched by the store detective.
Dancing in the moshpit when your partner collapses beside you.

Remember you have a point of entry A and an objective point B at the end.

These points are not given. Decide how these scenes will play out. Where do you enter and where do you arrive at your objective and what will that be?

METAPHORS AND SIMILES

We use the game 'Essences' {A group game built around metaphors} to become 'The D'Artagnan of Description', metaphorically speaking

> 'He looked about as inconspicuous as a tarantula on a slice of angel food cake' Raymond Chandler

Here is an exercise to help you write using the imagery of metaphor. But first let us define the difference between simile and metaphor.

SIMILE: A figure of speech in which two unalike things are compared to create a descriptive image usually using the word like. e.g. 'She was like a summer shower'

METAPHOR- a figure of speech in which two things which are literally unable to be compared and joined are, as a way of indicating the properties of the second belonging to the first. e.g. She is snowfall on a mountainside, He was a bullet train.

Simile is similar while Metaphor means it **is** that thing. 'She is like a rose' is a simile but 'She is a rose' is a metaphor.

EXERCISE 24 'ESSENCES'

This game can be played with as few as two people but it is best with four or more players. Each player needs to have a pen and paper. One player will announce to the others that he or she is thinking of a specific person and will offer up a brief clue to their identity- someone well known/universally famous or infamous. All the others will suggest 'metaphor possibilities' to the first player. The first player will use these to describe the person they are thinking of, as a metaphor. The other players will write down each example until they have built up a picture of the person based on the metaphors and are able to make an educated guess as to the identity of the person.

EXAMPLE

The first player says' I am thinking of a dead male American singer.'

Each of the others in turn will say things like, 'If he was a pair of shoes what would he be?' OR 'If he were a cake what would he be?'

The first player will reply by saying 'He is a pair of black leather gym boots.' OR 'He is a slice of Black Forest chocolate cake.'

The game may go on for several more metaphors but the answer to this one was Michael Jackson.

Our first player says, 'I am thinking of a dead European scientist.' And so that we can understand this game fully, let's be in the know. We know that he is thinking of Albert Einstein.

Now the second player might say, 'If he was an animal what would he be?'

If you were the first player how would you answer that? What kind of animal would Albert Einstein be?

Writer: How to write short stories, novellas and novels

The first player might reply 'He is a cocker spaniel.' Everyone jots down cocker spaniel on their sheet of paper.

The third player asks, 'If he were a drink what might he be?'

How would you answer that? Is Albert a German beer or is he a warm cup of tea? Or something else?

The next game, the answer is at the end, see if you can work it out.

First player: 'I am thinking of a dead American male entertainer.'

Second player: 'If he was a cigarette what would he be?'

First player: 'He is a hand rolled Cuban cigar'

Third player: 'If he was a shoe what would he be?'

First player:' He would be a black and white 1940s dancing shoe.'

Fourth player: 'If he was a hat, what would he be?'

First player: 'He would be a fedora.'

By now we are starting to build up a picture of someone with a sense of class and from a particular era.

Let's cut to the chase now.

Car: Cadillac

Drink: Whisky straight.

If you are getting close and think he might be an actor, you must write down on your paper who you think he is and then declare your last question by saying...

Second player- 'This is my last question; my Specific Metaphor question. If he were a film what would he be?'

Specific questions that are factual cannot be asked at the start. You can only ask a Specific Metaphor question that relates to the person in question, if you have accrued enough information to be sure.

IF YOU ARE WRONG IN YOUR GUESS YOU ARE OUT OF THE GAME.

Here the FIRST PLAYER must name a film he has been in.
First player- 'The Man with the Golden Arm.'

As it turns out this question was only to confirm what the second player knew and if you know your film history you would know the answer.

HOWEVER, IF YOU CAN GUESS THE PERSON BEFORE THE SPECIFIC METAPHOR QUESTION YOU ARE SUPERIOR IN THE GAME.

Second player- 'Is it Frank Sinatra?'

First player- 'Yes, it is Frank Sinatra.'

And that is how you play 'Essences'.

LANDSCAPE [AND NATURE] AS METAPHOR

The darkening sky, the rolling sea and other symbols of you and me

We are part of nature and are bound up in its' cycles and changes. Audiences enjoy being reminded of this and writers have used it constantly. When we use the sea or storms or gathering clouds or clear spring mornings or fields all wet with dew, we are connecting landscape and nature to mood and situation. It is a subtle way of adding emphasis to what we are trying to say about our main characters or their predicament. Shakespeare in 'Macbeth' sets up the world of nature as being out of kilter and haunted by Macbeth's crimes. In the second book of Susan Cooper's *'The Dark is Rising'* series she presages the coming horrors by using birds and trees and leaves all moving in unusual ways. The main character Will Stanton gradually becomes aware of these freak occurrences, that are subtle at first but become more pronounced and threatening.

EXERCISE 25

Write a passage in which your focal character moves through a landscape that clearly indicates mood and atmosphere. The location should reflect the psychological and emotional state of the protagonist.

Set your passage in:

- A particularly seedy part of a city, a criminal underworld district.
- The blossoming countryside full of fields and grain and orchards.
- A windswept uninhabited beach.
- An industrious dockside at sunrise.
- The same dockside at night as the bars are closing

CHAPTER TEN
STYLISTIC CONSIDERATIONS

[NOT] Making the Reader Conscious of Writing
Adverbs and Adjectives Ad Nauseaum
Avoiding or Embracing the Cliche
The Sin of Exposition
Exercise 26
Unstructured Writing
Breaking the Rules

[NOT] MAKING THE READER CONSCIOUS OF WRITING

Overly flowery writing vs lean and concise

Writers should be in love with storytelling and understand how to tell stories seamlessly. Some writers, even those not new to the craft, get swept up in the sound of words. Others write endlessly long sentences that they hold together using ands and commas.

Good writing should be a balance between the requisite pace and clear, concise imagery. In other words, you tell a story at the pace required to move your story along, you give it emotional and psychological tone and just enough description to create the correct mood. AND NOTHING MORE. [My opinion, you can disagree.]

However, there are other ways to write. If you read 19th century novels you will be struck by how 'word/sentence heavy' they are. Though the Bronte's, Dickens, Thomas Hardy and Gustave Flaubert all create wonderful stories full of powerful characters, their work is full of extensive and powerfully descriptive language. Much of it would appear dense; quite slow reading. This is not a bad thing but it is a great deal of work for both writer and reader. These works were written in a slower, less complex world in which reading was a major pastime. People saw reading, along with singing around the piano, as the main activity of an evening. They expected a story to be as rich with words as possible.

With the arrival of the 20th century writing takes on a more journalistic influence. The world is a faster place and the writers/novels/ kinds of writing serve a much faster lifestyle. There is more 'reportage', less descriptive overkill. Sometimes you get a very lean and spare kind of writing. Steinbeck and Hemingway are good examples of this.

He was an old man who fished alone in a skiff in the Gulf Stream and he had gone eighty-four days now without taking a fish. In the first forty days a boy had been with him. But after forty days without a fish the boy's parents had told him that the old man was now definitely and finally salao, which is the worst form of unlucky and the boy had gone at their orders in another boat which caught three good fish the first week. It made the boy sad to see the old man come in each day with his skiff empty and he always went down to help him carry either the coiled lines or the gaff and harpoon and the sail that was furled around the mast. The sail was patched with flour sacks and, furled; it looked like the flag of permanent defeat

The opening paragraph from 'The Old Man and the Sea' by Ernest Hemingway.

Some of the sentences do run on in this opening paragraph but the prose is not top heavy with too many adverbs and adjectives. It is easy to read and flows well.

Here is a more elaborate kind of writing from the 1800s.

London. Michaelmas term lately over and the Lord Chancellor sitting in Lincoln's Inn Hall. Implacable November weather. As much mud in the streets as if the waters had but newly retired from the face of the earth, and it would not be wonderful to meet a Megalosaurus, forty feet long or so, waddling like an elephantine lizard up Holborn Hill. Smoke lowering down from chimney-pots, making a soft black drizzle, with flakes of soot in it as big as full-grown snowflakes--gone into mourning, one might imagine, for the death of the sun. Dogs, undistinguishable in mire. Horses, scarcely better; splashed to their very blinkers. Foot passengers, jostling one another's umbrellas in a general infection of ill temper, and losing their foot-hold at street-corners, where tens of thousands of other foot passengers have been slipping and sliding since the day broke (if this day ever broke), adding new deposits to the crust upon crust of mud, sticking at those points tenaciously to the pavement, and accumulating at compound interest.

Fog everywhere. Fog up the river, where it flows among green aits and meadows; fog down the river, where it rolls defiled among the tiers of shipping and the waterside pollutions of a great (and dirty) city. Fog on the Essex marshes, fog on the Kentish heights. Fog creeping into the cabooses of collier-brigs; fog lying out on the yards and hovering in the rigging of great ships; fog drooping on the gunwales of barges and small boats. Fog in the eyes and throats of ancient Greenwich pensioners, wheezing by the firesides of their wards; fog in the stem and bowl of the afternoon pipe of the wrathful skipper, down in his close cabin; fog cruelly pinching the toes and fingers of his shivering little 'prentice boy on deck. Chance people on the bridges peeping over the parapets into a nether sky of fog, with fog all round them, as if they were up in a balloon and hanging in the misty clouds.

The opening paragraph from *'Bleak House'* by Charles Dickens.

Both authors exercise great control over these scenes. They make them live before your eyes. Decide how to tell your story and what works for you. Do not overwrite just for the sake of it, simply because you have fallen in love with the sound of words. Most authors talk about how they go back over their drafts and pare the words back.

However, some contemporary writers do engage in a more florid style and their audience is swept away, by the lyrical nature of their prose.

Angela Carter's work deals with sexuality, nature, the relationship between man, woman and animal, often within the context of well- known folktales. Her poetic style, with a heavy emphasis on imagery and poetic turns of phrase, is in keeping with the subject matter and themes. A more baroque style, can be useful, if the subject matter demands it.

Kate Forsyth covers similar ground in her books but has a less ornate approach to her writing. Whilst being beautifully descriptive it does not draw attention to itself with lyrical flourishes. Choose wisely! Know the difference between writing that serves style and theme and just plain overwriting.

George Orwell's Rule No. 2 for Writing.

"Never use a long word where a short one will do."

The words need to be in the service of the story and not the other way around.

IF YOU HAVE A COMPELLING STORY, POWERFUL CHARACTERS WRITTEN WITH A PACE AND RHYTHM THAT SUITS THE NARRATIVE THEN DON'T WEIGH IT DOWN WITH TOO MANY WORDS....OR TOO MANY OVERLONG SENTENCES.

AGAIN, ONE MORE WORD ABOUT OVERWRITING

Writers love words. Writers love ideas. Writers love characters and stories. Writers don't know when to shut up.

SO NOT OVERWRITING BUT REWORKING

Lazy writing is stories that have not been reworked. They are written by self -satisfied writers who believe that everything they write is gold! Often much of what they write is predictable, ordinary and imitative.

You will need to go back and shave off, reduce, simplify your story. Make your writing tighter, your characters more identifiable, your plotlines and turning points more believable, powerful and surprising. This is necessary for pace and rhythm, for clarity, for a dozen different reasons.

REWRITE! REWRITE! REWRITE!

ADVERBS AND ADJECTIVES AD NAUSEAUM

The fine art of description and when to know when enough is enough

Words need to serve the story. Plot and pace are far more important than description. Whenever you can, go through and delete the descriptors. Can you make your story clear without making it top heavy with adverbs and adjectives? If you see an adverb; one of those annoying 'ly' words, ask yourself do I need it? They are the most common baggage in a story. Will the story read better without it?

Soon you will start to see whole sentences that are unnecessary. Kill them off. It is the narrative flow that matters.

I am not saying don't use descriptors but rather to be sparing and in control.

Need further proof.

1940 London. Prime Minister Winston Churchill addresses his nation in its' darkest hour.

"We shall fight on the beaches, we shall fight on the landing grounds, we shall fight in the fields and in the streets, we shall fight in the hills; we shall never surrender."

Nothing but pronouns, nouns and verbs, not a single adjective or adverb to be seen. And all short words bar the last one.

Luca Collins

AVOIDING OR EMBRACING THE CLICHÉ

A word is worth a thousand pictures. Inverting clichés

*Meet Gillian, at 27 she is a woman with a career path and a **fire in the belly**. Meet Prue 32, Gillian's **right-hand woman**. Together they are design consultants for a large, successful architectural refurbishing company. Gillian **has tickets on herself**, she thinks she is **God's gift to** interior design – a bit of a big head.*

The one thing she hates is people mispronouncing her name. It is Gillian with a soft 'G' sound, like in Joseph. If she is called Gillian with a hard 'G' as in go, her stock reply is "What am I a fish?" with all the venom she can muster.

Already I have thrown in at least four clichés but this is no crime. They often serve as a kind of shorthand, that allows the reader to get to **the meat of the story** as quickly as possible. They are often called idiomatic speech. You can get away with this to a degree, since clichés appear so readily in natural conversation.

Situations and storylines, characters and conflicts are a different matter. Clichés used sparingly in language are forgivable, even necessary sometimes. But hackneyed characters and story ideas bore an audience and are too large to be incidental. **They stand out like dog's balls**. But clichés can be inverted, used in a new and different way.

Just as an aside, the presentation of this brief vignette has me, as the author, talking directly to you –i.e. *Meet Gillian etc* - this draws attention to the fact that I am telling a story. The purpose here is instruction, so the writing does not lose its' informational tone. Writing serving story and purpose; it is not unlike a story brief, as we are not trying to tell the whole story but rather give a thumbnail sketch to illustrate a point about clichés.

Gillian and Prue are assigned the refurbishment of the first of a string of department stores. ***A lot is riding on this*** *and the women's boss Freya Mills is **breathing down their necks**.* {We are up to six now}

The manager of the department store, set in a smaller provincial city, is our romantic interest a guy called Jack Pitt.

So now we have a set up. *The refurbishment will have its difficulties, which will throw Jack and Gillian together. There will be a strong attraction but gradually the project will run over budget and that hard-fought control that Gillian has will **slip through her fingers**.*

*Worse still, will be how talk is getting around that **they have become an item** and now everyone is shortening her name to fit with his-* yep, you guessed it....**Jack and Jill**. Here we have a truly classic cliché straight from nursery rhymes but reworked in, we hope, a humorous and novel way.

Like most romantic tales it will spiral down to accusation and recrimination and result in a separation. This is stock standard but here we need to be inventive with plotline, so as not to fall into obvious and unintended cliché.

If there is a rapprochement and if we do end on a romantic high note {expected but not necessarily a cliché} then we will have this.

There is a high hill, one they made love on before. They stand together holding hands. And their friends and family are gathered on the slope. The couple are dressed in blouses and lederhosen, as if from a nursery rhyme and of course the female celebrant is dressed as Mother Goose in a large Victorian bonnet. The aisle is lined with wooden buckets.

We might call this tale 'Fetching Water'.

The point is that you can get away with a little cliché in conversation BUT avoid it in your descriptive writing and be inventive in your story construction, story and character arc; so as not to fall into lazy {seen a million times} storytelling.

IF YOU USE A CLICHÉ THEN INVERT IT.

MAKE IT CLEVER! MAKE IT BOUNCE OFF THE PAGE WITH INVENTIVENESS!

THE SIN OF EXPOSITION

Getting to the point and making the facts known, in the most natural way possible. Being funky not clunky

TWO MEANINGS OF EXPOSITION:

Sometimes the word 'Exposition' is used to describe part of the STORY STRUCTURE. As in 'In the exposition we discovered that the main character had a fear of heights but had a scornful brother who was a pilot'.

Here we will use the term to mean an explanation, by way of conversation, that is obvious and clumsy and designed essentially to deliver information.

Although dialogue is needed to convey information, we must be careful not to write dialogue that is just exposition. In other words, two characters are talking in order to give information that is delivered in such an unnatural way, that it sounds like it came from a fact sheet or a documentary narration.

We have to work at getting information out without making it look laboured and unnatural.

Break the dialogue up.

Create enquiries and replies, comments and responses.

Place natural pauses and reaction sounds into replies such as 'mmm' 'Yes and' or 'Like' or 'You know'[last two are very teenage].

Place hedging in the dialogue – umms, aahs, stutters and link these to the emotional content of the conversation. Particularly if it is difficult or confusing then make your speaker hesitant in their delivery. BUT DON'T OVERDO IT!

Here is an example that has just the right balance-

'I..I wish I could make this easier' he stammered. 'I've always felt bad….bad about the way you ….you were treated in school Mel! But I've always been gutless. I hate confrontation!'.

This is only one way of writing the dialogue. You must develop an ear for natural conversation and be able to see when what you have written has a stilted and false sound to it.

What does normal natural dialogue sound like? Language often does not flow in complete sentences. There are sentences that are interrupted by cross talk, by the return fire of the other person and also by the first person themselves. This happens when that person hesitates, when they try to find the right words to say, when they are unsure of where they stand or where they are going with their conversation. Or where they are excited, getting ahead of themselves and their language cannot keep up with their thoughts.

Getting across information is probably the area in which dialogue can sound the most unnatural. Here you should try for the most natural and conversational of tones and allow for interjections and queries from the other participants. This serves to break up long passages of information into digestible morsels. Real life does not allow people to carry on with long winded explanations, sermonizing or poetic reveries. Usually someone will interrupt.

Develop an ear for the way language works. Study successful passages of dialogue in novels you have enjoyed. Photocopy passages and dissect them. Look at the intention within the conversation and how it was achieved.

EXERCISE 26

Create a scene between a doctor and a patient in which tragic news is conveyed.

- A long-haul truck driver has just picked up a pretty young girl hitch hiker. The old guy is protective and concerned that hitch hiking puts her at risk. She, on the other hand, has all the innocence and devil may care of youth.
- A husband has been unfaithful and feels he must convey it to his wife. She, up until this point has known nothing.
- Two girls, one older and one younger, sit in a playground and discuss the impending divorce of their parents. The younger is bewildered and the older tries to explain what will happen to them.
- A fortune teller tells a paying customer what lies in his future. He is anxious to find some good news in his life at this point.

UNSTRUCTURED WRITING?

Why you cannot just leave it the way you found it

{**Not** to be confused with **FREE WRITING** - which is a creative ideas exercise.}

Many novices believe that you just sit down with a pen or a keyboard and just begin to write and when you've finished the last word it is done [apart from some slight rejigging]. This implies that writing a brilliant, engaging story is no more difficult than telling an anecdote or writing a letter/email. Perhaps someone out there can do that but it's not me.

I am quite capable of writing a story that just flows from the pen or keyboard but that is not where it ends. I know that the larger and more complex it becomes the more I will need to look at all the aspects of story building. And even the small ones need reworking.

I need structure and I need to be able to balance dozens of different aspects of a complex, challenging story world. I am not that person that writes it once and it comes out perfect and I doubt if you are too.

As tedious as this might sound, you need to draw up plotlines, plot points, turning points, character arcs and story arcs to make the best story you can.

This may happen after you have written a treatment or it may be some of the preliminary work you do before embarking on the story. NONE OF THIS IS AT VARIENCE WITH THE 'AHA MOMENT'.

BREAKING THE RULES

Why iconoclasts have more fun

I love iconoclasts. I love stories that break the mould, that tell a story in a new and innovative way.

But in order, to break the rules, first you need to know the rules well and that only comes with years of practise. In truth, must *master the rules* before you are good enough to really break them.

CHAPTER ELEVEN
GENERAL HOUSEKEEPING

Short Story Writing
Tall Thoughts on Short Stories
Novellas
What Shall I Read?
Do Not Disturb the Dead my Child
Of Their Times
Investigative Principles
How Much Should I Write?
Ten Thousand Hours
A Personal Style
Here at the Western World
The Writer's Best Friend is a Log
The Writer's Best Friend is a Dog
You Only Get One Shot so Make it Count
And In The End
Hello I Must Be Going

SHORT STORY WRITING

The five elements of story writing revisited in short form

The most obvious thing about a short story is that it almost always obeys the rules of structure, character development and writing techniques that her big brother the novel does.

However, it may use archetypes and sometimes familiar settings in its first act as a way of getting to the story centre quickly.

The second act creates predicaments that are often unusual and unpredictable and yet are coherent.

Its third act can end with a resolution that is unexpected – a little twist.

A short story contains five elements that are common to novellas and novels.

Character

Short stories are peopled with sufficient characters to move the action along. There will be principal characters and some secondary characters but they will not have as deep a backstory as those in a novella or novel. Nor will they be as complex. Often characters will be archetypal as a form of shorthand, to let the audience know where the story is headed.

Setting

The setting is often chosen to be easily recognisable. However, some work is done by the author to familiarise the audience with unusual or fantastical settings. For example, dystopian societies in Sci-Fi or unfamiliar settings for Crime often need some elaboration.

Plot

The plot of a short story generally makes brief and concise statements to set up Act 1 and moves into the Complication [Act 2] very quickly. Short stories often rely on a twist at the end, one that the audience is truly surprised by. The Resolution [Act 3] has that moment where the audience is pleased or shocked by a strange turn of events or an unforseen development. The ending comes quickly and resolutely.

Conflict

Without conflict we have no action story. All action stories rely on opposing forces. Sometimes it will be another character that faces off against our principal character. Other times our principal character may be pitted against nature or fate or sometimes in a psychological drama they may face their own values and ideas, their own family or the expectations and controlling forces of their community or their own personal demons. {See previous CONFLICT section Chapter Six}

Theme

The theme is the central idea or belief in a short story. It is often as simple as Success or Failure/The Power of Self Belief/Love Wins/Life or Fate is cruel. A short story does not have room for a lot of themes so there are very few Secondary Themes.

TALL THOUGHTS ON SHORT STORIES

Never underestimate the little guy

Do not underestimate the power and importance of the short story. If you want to see how great this form can be then try the short stories of some of the masters – Edgar Allen Poe, Mark Twain, Guy de Maupassant, Ray Bradbury, O. Henry, Raymond Carver and Daphne Du Maurier.

Many novice writers think that they are short changing themselves and their readers by not writing a weighty doorstopper. They also feel that they will not be taken seriously if they do not write something as huge as 'War and Peace'. Nonsense! If you care more about your craft and less about fame and fortune, then you will use the short story as a way of becoming a great writer.

Short stories, by their very nature, force you to focus in on what is most important within storytelling. When you have become adept at this form you will start to see that often larger works are made up of a series of smaller tales that are embedded in the larger storyline. There are a number of such complete stories within the early chapters of *"The Lord of the Rings'*. The meeting with Tom Bombadil and the dream like occurrences on the barrow downs are two examples. Take the challenge of writing clearly and concisely, in the smaller form and see where it leads.

NOVELLAS

Just what on earth is a novella?

It is a narrative prose form that exists somewhere between a short story and a novel and like the short story contains the five essential elements - character, setting, plot, conflict and theme. Ian McEwan wrote, a novella is 'something that is between 20,000 and 40,000 words, long enough for a reader to inhabit a world or a consciousness and be kept there, short enough to be read in a setting or two and for the whole structure to be held in mind at first encounter.' *Notes on The Novella* – 2012 article *The New Yorker*.

It is perhaps the next stepping stone for the blossoming author. And as McEwan points out you are in illustrious company. *The Turn of The Screw* by Henry James, *Metamorphosis* by Franz Kafka, *Of Mice and Men* by John Steinbeck, *L'Etranger* by Albert Camus are all novellas.

A little general housekeeping now!

WHAT SHALL I READ?

Leave no page unturned

Basically, everything but make it diverse. Want to write a specific genre? Then look at what writers in that genre do. Apply a set of **Investigative Principles** to your genre and once you have digested the best then move on to new fields. Begin to read other kinds of fiction- historical, character studies, romance, mystery, urban crime. Also read fiction from other cultures because they offer new insights into how human beings behave and see the world. The more well-read you are the less you will be inclined to copy the genre masters and mistresses you have studied. Coming back to your genre preference after reading other genres, will free you up to be less influenced and less derivative. If you were writing fantasy fiction begin with Tolkien and Ursula Le Guinn but then perhaps go to Jane Austen, Raymond Chandler and Fennimore Cooper. Having come out the other side, you will begin to write with clear and non-rigid approaches to your craft.

DO NOT DISTURB THE DEAD MY CHILD

Do not be possessed by the dead [writers]

Throughout this book I have extolled the insights to be gained from the great writers of the past. But we also need to be aware of being too greatly influenced by those same writers. Each of them wrote for the audience of their time and you want to write for yours also. You need to write your concerns, your fears and visions into sophisticated literature that addresses, however obliquely, the challenges of your world.

Sometimes you can and do co-opt the style of a particular writer in order to capture the mood their books set. There have been a number of authors who have taken the characters and settings of a famous body of work and created a new volume. Here you are very consciously using their style but always to your own ends. You are still making it your own. For a truly brilliant reinterpretation in this manner, look at Kenneth Grahame's *'Wind in the Willows'* and then read its sequel *'The Willows in Winter'* by William Horwood, the author of *'Duncton Wood'*.

OF THEIR TIME

The 'N' Word and other 'social inappropriates', then and now

Here in the 21st Century many freedoms and changes in attitude have been, at least partially, won for those who once found themselves oppressed. And while we still have a great deal to do there have been great improvements, in the social conditions and the expectations of many minorities and disadvantaged groups.

However, there has been, in these politically correct times, a disturbing tendency to either rewrite or remove some of the great works of literature from circulation or at least to be critical of them for perceived or definite anti-Semitism, sexism, racism and homophobia and for creating women characters who live without any personal power or self-determination.

I would argue that Flaubert or Thomas Hardy create women who are disempowered in a man's world and who pay the ultimate price, precisely because that was the kind of world those women found themselves in. And it is precisely the injustice and tragedy of their circumstances that these writers set out to illuminate.

There can be little doubt that the narrator of *'Heart of Darkness'* sees those native inhabitants of the Congo River as inferior and when he describes some as 'nigger-fools' he is displaying all the inherent racism that British Empire builders displayed throughout 400 years of imperialism. And while his condescending manner probably barely raised an eyebrow, at the time of publication, it is highly offensive now. The same can be said of anti-Semitism in Shakespeare, Dickens and

'Ivanhoe' by Sir Walter Scott, to name but a few examples. Yet all three authors create fully realised Jewish characters that elicit our sympathy.

Do we ban these works for their inappropriateness to our own time or do we see them in the context of their times? If we react with a knee jerk response do we risk missing the author's intent?

Joseph Conrad's intent I believe was to make some comment on relations between white men and the inhabitants of the Congo. The use of 'nigger' in *'Huckleberry Finn'* is just as deliberate and purposeful. Jim, the runaway slave, may well be a figure of fun in the eyes of Huck, but our sympathies shift towards him as the narrative progresses and his treatment rankles. This is precisely what Twain intends.

Strong, empowered women nowadays find the heroine of Daphne De Maurier's *'Rebecca'* a weak ineffectual 'milk sop' of a girl. Would the story have worked in modern times? Possibly but it would have been a very different kind of heroine and story. Nonetheless, the novel was embraced by the women of her time and they must have seen, within the tale, something of themselves and possibly their own situation.

I believe it is important to appraise books within the context of the era in which they were written. Of course, we can compare and contrast them with our modern era and probably be grateful that we are not their contemporaries. But we must not dismiss them for being out of step with times fifty, a hundred, two hundred or more years ahead of their inception.

INVESTIGATIVE PRINCIPLES

What are we looking for in others' writing?

One way of both learning what other writers do and having some control over your own writing, is to ask questions about their style. Look specifically at aspects of the writing that make them individual and of their times.

How does the writer use landscape as metaphor? For a wonderful example of this go to the corn harvesting scene [Chapter 14] and in contrast, the rutabaga harvest scene [Chapter 43] in *'Tess of the D'Urbervilles'*.

How does the writer build up character and obsession? Obsession in the main character is often the driving force of the narrative. In Herman Melville's *'Moby Dick'*, it is Captain Ahab's fixation on the 'white whale' that leads to catastrophe and death. The unnamed heroine of Daphne du Maurier's *'Rebecca'* is obsessed with the seemingly perfect presence of her husband's dead wife, who haunts the newlyweds' home.

How does the writer build anticipation, a sense of foreboding, of dread in both characters and settings? Are there indicators, forewarnings, previous incidents, whispers and suggestions from secondary characters? For this, look no further than the chilling first chapters of Bram Stoker's *'Dracula'*.

How do the dialogue, thoughts and realisations of a particular character add to and illuminate that character? That internal dialogue and how it reveals character is particularly potent in Daniel Keyes *'Flowers for Algernon'*. Thoughts, dreams, half remembered glimpses of guilty incidents and memories all inform and drive this narrative.

How has the author used the structure of stories to create an innovative new way of presenting the story. Where does the narrative begin? Does it travel backwards or forwards from its beginning? How does the arrangement of acts reveal the action and character development within the text? John Fowles'-*'The Magus'* is a book that plays with structure and perceptions of reality to torment the main protagonist and intrigue the reader.

How is language used to convey character? Here there are literally thousands of examples. Look at dialogue and patois and regional accents as a way of delineating character. For this go to *'Huckleberry Finn'* By Mark Twain and the language of both Huck and Jim. Another brilliant example of language used to capture a changing character can be found in *'Flowers for Algernon'* by Daniel Keyes. In which a character goes from language used by a six year old to that of a super mind in the space of months but only a few hundred pages in this award winning book.

How is the writing presented in order to create action? Look at the pace and rhythm and how that ebbs and flows in and out of action and character scenes. For a truly wonderful example of this read Ernest Hemingway's prize winning novella *'The Old Man and the Sea'*.

How does the story resolve and does the ending bring to a justifiable and satisfying conclusion all the composite parts. Does that ending have the appropriate resonance to complete the tone of the story. For brief examples of endings see AND IN THE END and then begin the study of these texts and see how the stories and their endings complement each other.

This is part of your calling – to read and absorb these authors and to understand how they did what they did; to make those insights part of your own vocabulary as a writer.

Build up a list of INVESTIGATIVE PRINCIPLES of your own as you develop your knowledge.

HOW MUCH SHOULD I WRITE?

A kilo of kreativity kontinually!

As children, we learn by imitation and so it is as writers. Do not worry initially if your work reminds you of other people. That will change. The important thing is to keep writing – but how much? The generally accepted minimum is **ONE THOUSAND WORDS A DAY.**
That is every day.
Make sure you have a clean, uninterrupted space to use and return to, with a door that can shut out the world. No radios or TVs - though music is often helpful. I suggest instrumental rather than lyric driven. Turn your phone to message bank. Have a comfortable chair and decent size desk, with a bright reading lamp for night and hopefully a ventilated window for days.
You should have a dictionary and thesaurus plus any reference books you will need within close reach, as well as pens and paper. I know you are thinking but all of this is on my computer. Fine, but computers crash SO HAVE BOOKS NEARBY AND back up regularly- about every thirty minutes.
And when that computer eventually crashes you need to continue the old fashion way. Yes, one thousand words every day and technical malfunction is no excuse. Is it Hal?

TEN THOUSAND HOURS

Do you really want to be a writer?

One thousand words is one way to look at it but there is also this way. Time spent researching, thinking, reworking already written passages is also writing so perhaps hours rather than word count is the way to go.

There is an anecdote that goes, that someone asked Thomas Keneally how you become a writer? His reply was, "It's easy, all you have to do is write for a minimum of four hours a day and in ten years you will be a writer".

We said we must write every day but let's suppose that there will be a number of days when you cannot write, when you are sick or someone else is, you are travelling between destinations, a wedding, family gatherings etc. Let us take out 65 days for these contingencies.

For three hundred days, you put in the requisite four hours and have 1200 hours clocked up each year. In just under ten years you will have fulfilled the ten thousand hours to have mastered a discipline.

The question you should ask yourself is – 'Do I really want to be a writer?' Ten thousand hours will make you an accomplished guitarist, a proficient soccer player, a fabulous tango dancer, really almost anything in the world where a skill can be taught.

The burning question is - Do you burn also? Do you burn inside to tell stories? Are they unstoppable? Do they haunt your sleeping and waking hours?

If the answer is yes then we have not been wasting our time here. If the answer is no then ten thousand hours will probably get you a gold medal at the Olympics, in Greco-Roman Wrestling. Good Luck!

A PERSONAL STYLE

Hitting the Mark when never the Twain shall meet

How do we develop a personal style? Not an easy one to answer but certainly part of it is to take what you like from others and make it your own. But also remember there is no-one who sees the world the way that you do, so celebrate that uniqueness in your writing. Enjoy your idiosyncrasies and quirks. Readers and publishers are looking for a unique new voice and not a copy of what went before.

It is a difficult balancing act learning from the masters and finding your own voice. Be patient. It will come but only with practise and sad to say with any number of early failures. So, a thousand words a day as a minimum but probably a hundred or more failures or near misses before you hit the mark.

Although hitting the mark might be what your appreciative audience calls it, you may not feel that way. Expect to be disappointed. You will write ever improving work if you keep at it but, if you are striving to say something worthwhile, you will often feel that you didn't quite get there. Stories are not just the amalgam of their composite parts. They are observations and slow reveals of the human condition. If you are an acute observer of people you will try to capture our essence, a truth in your storytelling and may feel you have found only part of it. Have faith and keep writing.

HERE AT THE WESTERN WORLD

A look at the occidental, the oriental and the 'Other'

Here in the western world, where the Grimm's and Anderson's fairytales have been Disneyfied, stories do not serve the purpose they once did; they have been altered and reduced in power. The necessity to sell popcorn means that stories end most often with a neat often positive resolution. We create illusions that deny reality and deep inside we know it.

When we travel amongst the noise and clatter of the developing world we remind ourselves that we can fly out, at a moment's notice. Our passport and wealth allow us an escape route denied to the locals. Back home, faced with life threatening diseases, we expect technology, medicine and first world governments to cocoon us from the realities of the rest of the world.

We demand health, long life, success, acknowledgement, order, justice, transparency, social organisation, accountability and safety from our world. We return home, close the doors, light and warm our houses and believe the outside world will stand still while we sleep peacefully till morn.

Deep inside we know that the ground we stand on is not stable, that the sky above can change to force ten catastrophe, that our fortunes can vanish with the next financial crisis. We get a glimpse into that place when we enter the world of the 'Other'. That world is peopled with the exotic, with the alluring, passionate, beguiling, mystical and fascinating. But is also peopled with the uncomprehending, the violent, fanatical, warring and the self-serving.

We fall into the world of the 'Other' willingly. Sometimes the world of the 'Other' is just one mistake away- on the other side of midnight, across the railway tracks, around the corner from that wrong turn.

The 'Other' has held a fascination for us since the first explorers came back with tales of the places we had never been – Cathay, El Dorado, Timbuktu.

Authors understand this desire and obsession. Joseph Conrad's *'Heart of Darkness'* is written around a trip up the Congo River. It creates a world that goes from the everyday into a world of obsession and megalomania.

Now in our international, twenty four hour connected world some of those places and people are no longer as 'other worldly' as they once were. Now we need to turn familiar worlds upside down. We need to give places a new and original twist. Or we need to create more fantastic worlds or more exotic times in order to create that sense of wonder. That is one of your challenges. Look at what contemporary writers have done to create that otherness. One fabulous example is the book *'Life of Pi'* by Yann Martel, in which various interpretations of reality make the improbable and the almost impossible seem real.

But be aware of clichés and conventional first world takes on the OTHER. Africa is not a country it is [at this moment], 54 countries all with different cultures, customs, religions and languages. It is no more the land of Tarzan than The Famous Five represents England. Real empathy and research is needed. And nothing beats actually living where your story is set. Failing that, talk to those who have lived there, especially those whose families go back generations. For a brilliant insight into this go to the TED TALKS online, Ten Writers on Writing – Chimamanda Ngozi Adichie: The danger of a single story.

A WRITER'S BEST FRIEND IS A LOG

Write now! Right now!

It can be a tablet or a smartphone or a pocket book but somewhere to jot down story ideas, scraps of dialogue, observations, inspiring quotes, descriptive prose, dreams and important facts is essential to every writer.

Get it down. Do not believe that you can rely on memory sometime later. If you are driving pull over...if it arrives in a dream then wake up and write it down.

Once an observation or idea has been committed to text in some form then something amazing begins to happen- other associated ideas will gather looking to link up. There can be hours of creativity that arrive at the most inopportune moments, for this process has no respect for time or place or the inconvenience it causes. Many of the associated benefits {those expansive ideas waiting in the wings} will not be there later. What you write afterwards will not necessarily have the power and promise that writing made in the moment of inspiration has.

A WRITER'S BEST FRIEND IS A DOG

Why 'Walkies' is a literary boon

Writing is a solitary process and sometimes it can be a little lonesome. Having a dog with you can give you the company you desire. They will sit patiently by your desk for hours, oblivious to all you are going through, waiting for those magic words, ' *Come on Shakespeare let's go for a walk!*'.

Here's where dogs beat cats, parakeets and toads hands down. Hard to put a leash on a goldfish. On that walk, you can create that all important dialogue exchange, unlock the complexity of a character or solve that plot conundrum. And 'Cujo' or 'Baskerville' will be right there wagging a tail of approval for your brilliant efforts. Never underestimate the value of a walk with your first and most appreciative of audiences – the mutt.

YOU ONLY GET ONE SHOT SO MAKE IT COUNT

That opening salvo, the one that will grab them and shake them

The room came back into the light. It stank of spilt wine, nicotine and a whiff of carbolic acid. In his stupor, he stumbled toward the bathroom tripping over her legs, as she lay asleep in the armchair.

'Sorry!', he shot out before wrapping his hand tightly across his mouth. He gripped the bowl and heaved the greater part of four bottles of Bordeaux Cabernet and three courses into the blue water. Mid retch he stopped and crawled back to the door. It couldn't be?

There were those beautiful legs, running up to that figure hugging dress and that face staring blankly, no longer promising impossible pleasure but twisted and gone. She had been dead for a number of hours.

It was the last day of her summer vacation and although she had to pack, she hung out for one final moment on the dunes beside the grey Atlantic, hidden from view. And there he was again, the old man with the dewlap bag, weighed down, struggling, disappearing into the forest behind. She knew he was doing something that he didn't want others to see; the same as yesterday and last Wednesday. But what?

The dog was just a mongrel but so full of joy and gymnastic bounce that he was difficult to ignore. The dog and the boy. The beggar boy held out his hand for alms. Paul placed three coins in his palm, not knowing their worth. The boy smiled and handed him a business card. "THERE IS ONLY ONE WAY TO SOLVE IT" was all it said.'

Three possible starts to three unwritten stories. Did they get you in? Did they create wonder and questions?

Publishers receive thousands, if not tens of thousands, of manuscripts every year. You have moments to sell it to them before they move on. Many read the first sentence and stop there. Others will give you a paragraph. Some may give a page but rarely more.

One great opening sentence, leading to a great paragraph, leading to an arresting first page - a page full of questions, puzzles, mysteries, emotive moments, interesting characters, threatening situations.

You need to convince them that they are in for a great read – this will be worth it! But you only get one chance.

AND IN THE END

The final sentence/paragraph and all that it encompasses

Now that you have the attention of that initial publisher or the reader and have created a well-rounded and engaging story, you need to resolve it in the best way possible. The final paragraph and especially the final sentence must complement the characteristics of your story. The ending can be ironic or bittersweet, nostalgic or regretful. It may present a revelation that surprises but makes cogent sense. It may suggest that the story is unresolved and that we are still left within the heart of a mystery. It may be full of political and social observation. It may represent a resolution of life's tribulations and a life affirming ending. It may end bleakly with all the sadness and horror that the story carried throughout. Whatever the ending, it must be a true encapsulation of the facets of the story. In music, from songs to symphonies, they often end with a coda, that brings to finality the themes within the musical piece and your ending must do the same for your story.

Here are some of the endings to some short stories, novellas and novels. Part of your task as a developing writer will be to read these works and to ask yourself how these endings fulfil their roles and meet the demands of character, plot and intention?

Max stepped into his private boat and waved goodbye and sailed back over a year and in and out of weeks and through a day and into the night of his very own room where he found his supper waiting for him- and it was still hot.

Where the Wild Things Are – Maurice Sendak

And I have by me, for my comfort, two strange white flowers- shrivelled now, and brown and flat and brittle – to witness that even when mind and strength had gone, gratitude and mutual tenderness still lived on in the heart of man.

The Time Machine- H. G. Wells

Where was the Judge whom he had never seen? Where was the High Court, to which he had never penetrated? He raised his hands and spread out all his fingers.

But the hands of one of the partners were already at K.'s throat, while the other thrust the knife into his heart and turned it there twice. With failing eyes K. could still see the two of them, cheek leaning against cheek, immediately before his face, watching the final act. 'Like a dog!' he said: it was as if he meant the shame of it to outlive him.

The Trial – Franz Kafka

'We are friends,' said I, rising and bending over her, as she rose from the bench.

'And will continue friends apart,' said Estella.

I took her hand in mine, and we went out of that ruined place; and as the morning mists had risen long ago when I first left the forge, so now the evening mists were rising now, and in all the broad expanse of the tranquil light they showed to me, I saw no shadow of another parting from her.

Great Expectations – Charles Dickens

'...when they finally saw him, why he hadn't done any of those things... Atticus, he was real nice...'

His hands were under my chin, pulling up the cover, tucking it around me.

'Most people are, Scout, when you finally see them.'

He turned out the light and went into Jem's room. He would be there all night, and he would be there when Jem waked up in the morning.

To Kill a Mocking Bird – Harper Lee

"I lingered round them under that benign sky; watched the moths fluttering among the heath, and hare-bells; listened to the soft wind breathing through the grass; and wondered how anyone could ever imagine unquiet slumbers for the sleepers in that quiet earth."

Wuthering Heights – Emily Bronte

But wherever they go, and whatever happens to them on the way, in that enchanted place on the top of the Forest, a little boy and his Bear will always be playing.

The House at Pooh Corner – A.A. Milne

A LAST NOTE FROM THE NARRATOR. *I am haunted by humans.*

The Book Thief – Markus Zusak.

Most of the big shore places were closed now and there were hardly any lights except the shadowy, moving glow of a ferryboat across the Sound. And as the moon rose higher the inessential houses began to melt away until gradually I became aware of the old island here that flowered once for Dutch *sailors' eyes—a fresh, green breast of the new world. Its vanished trees, the trees that had made way for Gatsby's house, had once pandered in whispers to the last and greatest of all human dreams; for a transitory enchanted moment man must have held his breath in the presence of this continent, compelled into an æsthetic contemplation he neither understood nor desired, face to face for the last time in history with something commensurate to his capacity for wonder.*

And as I sat there, brooding on the old unknown world, I thought of Gatsby's wonder when he first picked out the green light at the end of Daisy's dock. He had come a long way to this blue lawn and his dream must have seemed so close that he could hardly fail to grasp it. He did not know that it was already behind him, somewhere back in that vast obscurity beyond the city, where the dark fields of the republic rolled on under the night.

Gatsby believed in the green light, the orgastic future that year by year recedes before us. It eluded us then, but that's no matter—tomorrow we will run faster, stretch out our arms farther.... And one fine morning——So we beat on, boats against the current, borne back ceaselessly into the past.

The Great Gatsby – F. Scott Fitzgerald

I dont no why Im dumb agen or what I did rong. Mabye its because I dint try hard enuf or just some body put the evel eye on me. But if I try and practis very hard mabye I'll get a littel smarter and no what all the words are. I remembir a littel bit how nice I had a feeling with the blue book that I red with the toren cover. And when I close my eyes I think about the man who tored the book and he looks like me only he looks different and be talks different but I dont think its me because its like I see him from the window. Anyway thats why Im gone to keep trying to get smart so I can have that feeling agen. Its good to no things and be smart and I wish I new evrything in the hole world. I wish I coud be smart agen rite now. If I coud I woud sit down and reed all the time.

Anyway I bet Im the frist dumb persen in the world who found out some thing inportent for sience. I did somthing but I dont remembir what. So I gess its like I did it for all the dumb pepul like me in Warren and all over the world. Goodby Miss Kinnian and dr Strauss and evrybody...

P.S. please tel prof Nemur not to be such a grouch when pepul laff at him

and he woud have more frends. Its easy to have fiends if you let pepul laff

at you. Im going to have lots of fiends where I go.

P.S. please if you get a chanse put some flowrs on Algernons grave in the bakyard.

Flowers for Algernon – Daniel Keyes

HELLO I MUST BE GOING!

A brief look at all we have covered….. We have come a long way

Again, let me emphasize that you might begin your writing career with short stories. Short stories are everything that we have studied and learnt but in miniature. We can see what we are trying to create, without getting lost in the magnitude of trying to tell a saga.

Short stories are a great way to refine your knowledge and your skills before tackling something as demanding as a novella or a novel.

Good luck!

SO LET ME INTODUCE TO YOU…

Our journey is only part way there for those who wish to write Fantasy Fiction. And for those of you who don't, may I suggest there is still much to learn from The Hero's Journey that will still apply to Contemporary Fiction. So let us travel on…

WRITER II.
How to Write Fantasy Fiction using the Hero's Journey
Luca Collins

INTRODUCTION

'All stories consist of a few common structural elements found universally in myths, fairytales, dreams and movies. They are known collectively as the Hero's Journey'

Christopher Vogler – 'The Writer's Journey

What Writer II offers and a brief introduction to those who blazed the trail

Writer II is a technical information section that gives you an overview of how 'The Hero's Journey' works. Obviously, it applies to the writing of Fantasy Fiction but it can also apply to realist fiction as well. This blueprint applies to contemporary as well as 'classic' fiction- the greats of the Western Canon. But a basic knowledge of the building blocks of novels, novellas and short stories is a necessity for applying this schema. To that end, it is absolutely imperative to understand those concepts found in Writer I.

Imaginative or Fantasy Fiction has particular characteristics but covers a very broad spectrum. The genre includes the originators, such as Aesop, Homer, Jonathan Swift, Edgar Allan Poe, Robert Louis Stevenson, The Grimm Brothers, Charles Perrault and Jules Verne. It then follows with consolidators of the style including H.G. Wells, Tolkien, Kenneth Grahame, C.S. Lewis, Aldous Huxley and George Orwell. It continues with latter twentieth century innovators in the form of Ray Bradbury, Philip K. Dick, Ursula Le Guinn and J.K. Rowling to name just some of the writers within the form.

What possible connection do this disparate group have with fantasy fiction? Can horror stories, political satires, dystopian fiction, science fiction, fantasy adventures, folktales, anthropomorphic tales, legends and myths all sit comfortably together? What they all have in common is that the stories, while some may be based on the real world, are not set in the real world but their reality is as solid as it is fantastical.

By using the tools of storytelling, the type that a writer of realist fiction would use, authors are able to create worlds, in which the most unlikely of creatures and situations have believability. When they create fantastical worlds, they create works that comment on and reflect our world. Frodo Baggins, Dr Jekyll, Mr Toad and Winston Smith are as real to the reader as Holden Caulfield or Tom Joad, Tess of the D'Urbervilles or David Copperfield.

REFERENCING BOOKS AND FILMS

The printed page and silver screen and how they illuminate each other

At times examples from particular writers and specific literary characters and situations are cited but for expediency, scenes and characters from films are also quoted. Films provide a quick and easily accessible way to grasp an idea that is being presented. We are moving into an era in which we are becoming {if we have not already become} as visually literate as we are with what is on the written page. Whatever is seen on the screen was once on the page, as a screenplay and therefore meets many of the same demands and is bounded by the same parameters, as the novel and the short story. Many films were novels and short stories first and then screenplays.

What is being presented here is only the surface of a deep and profound schema for understanding story. If you wish to use this approach you will need to delve even more deeply into the psychological ramifications of 'The Hero's Journey'. Much is available on the web but Joseph Campbell and Christopher Vogler are essential reading.

CHAPTER ONE
THE BASICS

Defining Hero for the writer and the reader
The Hero's story in many forms
The Archetypes
The Hero
The Meaning of Hero
Order, Punishment and Fate [Disorder]
The Meaning of Sacrifice
Anti-Hero
Hero and Villain
Character Flaws
The Importance of being Ordinary
Catalyst Hero
Tragic Hero

DEFINING HERO

Let us be clear from the start, that the word 'Hero' is treated the same as poet or doctor or even soldier. It is neither male nor female but refers to both. For the sake of brevity and to keep focus we are going to deal mostly with fantasy fiction and fantasy film and therefore the image and concept of hero will constantly appear but always as gender non- specific.

Writer II will alternate between 'he' and 'she' and will use 'they' to imply both.

THE HERO'S STORY IN MANY FORMS

More than folktale, myth or legend

The hero is not always bound to a traditional storyline. The possibilities within these journey stories are limitless. Yes, we will still have tales about defeating enemies, saving the captive and winning the prize but hero stories can take many forms.

It might be a story of survival, of passing through the wasteland, facing its trials and arriving safely at some promised point. John Wyndham's science fiction classic *'The Chrysalids'* is an example of this kind of story.

It may be the story of a personal loss that our principal character needs to come to terms with- *'Looking for Alaska'* by John Green is an example of this, from realist fiction and similarly *'Bridge to Terabithia'* by Katherine Paterson is another example, involving a mix of realist and fantasy fiction. Or a journey involving the gaining of knowledge and wisdom, in which our main character meets those with something to offer. Often, he or she will make poor choices and find themselves on the wrong side of the law, in danger, poorer than they were before, hoodwinked and abandoned. These calamities allow our hero the chance to learn and grow. Any number of Dickens' novels follow this story arc. The final story may be an amalgam of all these and more.

Study hero tales from many eras and cultures and decide what kind of story *you* want to tell.

THE ARCHETYPES

Archetypes not Stereotypes

The archetypes that appear within myths and legends, fairy and folktales serve as signposts within your story. By signposts I mean that they indicate positions along the story continuum, what kind of situation the protagonist has entered and what newly arrived characters represent, in terms of help or threat. **The archetypes are both narrative positions and character aspects – they are story functions.**

While these universal archetypes have existed in storytelling since the beginning, we are not locked into a set of predictable forms. With imagination, we can create a multitude of characters and situations by mixing and matching these archetypes, for example - A Shapeshifter may well be a Mentor and an Ally, as easily as it might be a Herald or a Shadow Villain. And it has arrived at a point in the story, where the presence of a Shapeshifter serves a specific purpose, a function within the story. This may not make sense now but it will.

Archetypes exist within your characters but they are not characters themselves. **They are *Archetypes* used *within characters* and *not Stereotypes as characters*.**

In other words, your characters need to be three dimensional and not cardboard cut-outs. Any character may take on or dispense with more than one archetype, in the course of a story. Sometimes they may exhibit a number of archetypes at the same time. As we travel through the archetypes see them as aspects of character – they will appear within your heroes, villains, mentors, love interests, companions and all the other fully fleshed out characters you have created.

Although there is no strict order in which Archetypes will appear in a Hero's Journey narrative, the archetypes here are placed in as logical an order as possible. Usually you would meet a Herald and a Mentor early in a story while it is more likely that Shadows, Shapeshifters and Villains will appear later - in other words, they appear within *a linear three act structure* at reasonably natural points, in story development. Here I am presenting *the narrative in its' traditional form.*

You can, however, rearrange the elements of your story to place the characters and incidents in new and innovative arrangements. {See Writer I. The Three Act Structure Reworked –Frankenstein}

THE HERO

Order

The Hero represents the journey back to restoration, from an initial stage of dislocation. It is a search for order in society, for completeness of personality. Heroes are participating in a journey, which will test them and finally [usually] reward them and their community. Their world has been thrown off balance and they must restore it to order, perhaps the order that it originally had or a new order greatly improved. But equally it is about wholeness of self.

Punishment and Fate {Disorder}

Some of the more fatalistic tales do not restore order in a modern sense instead the hero suffers and fails.

'*Daedalus and Icarus*' and '*Theseus*' are examples from Greek Mythology.

King Minos of Crete fails to give proper sacrifice to the Gods and as punishment his wife falls in love with a beautiful white bull, originally the gift of Poseidon. She gives birth to the Minotaur, a half- man half- bull that can only be sated by the sacrifice of Athenian youth, seven boys and seven girls. Daedalus an ingenious inventor is ordered to build a labyrinth to hold the monster.

The warrior Theseus, takes the place of one of the young men, kills the beast and escapes the labyrinth with the aid of both Daedalus and Ariadne, the king's daughter, who has fallen in love with him. Theseus and Ariadne flee and angered over this deception King Minos throws Daedalus and his son Icarus into the labyrinth. But Daedalus builds wings for them to escape the maze. Ignoring his father's warnings, Icarus flies too close to the sun melting his wings and plummets into the sea.

Theseus is told by the Goddess Athena he must leave Ariadne behind and so he sails for home. He had promised his father to change his black sails to white to indicate his success but grieving over the loss of Ariadne he forgets to give the order. His father seeing the black sails from his palace and believing his son dead, hurls himself into the sea.

The only order that can be found in all of this is that of the Gods. All have been punished for the failure to show due homage to those on Mt Olympus.

Twenty first century heroes are usually expected, against all odds, to bring order. This is particularly true in Western

Americanized cultures. We no longer see ourselves as being subject to the whims of fate or the hands of the Gods.

A hero needs to be universally recognised by the readership but sufficiently original enough for them to feel that this is not someone that they have seen too many times before.

THE MEANING OF SACRIFICE

Whilst heroes set out on a journey full of dangerous tasks, it is sacrifice that is the most powerful factor in fantasy storytelling. It is a particularly strong principle of mainstream writing also. Each hero must be prepared to risk their own safety; to sacrifice their previous sense of themselves and ultimately, if necessary, their own life.

Heroes accept that they will put their lives on the line. {See references to 'A Tale of Two Cities' and Severus Snape in **Irony W 1**.}

Sacrifice in story terms is seen as - 'The Death of the Ego'. This is a transcendent state in which heroes have stepped beyond the earthbound needs and desires of common men and women.

Entering the moment of sacrifice and possible death, perception, awareness and understanding all change here. The hero becomes super aware of both themselves and the world around them. Realizations occur, hidden truths are revealed to the hero and an understanding of the greater scheme of things may appear.

THE CHANGING NATURE OF HEROES

Heroes in ancient myth and legends are strong and resourceful but in many cultures, they can also be the playthings of the gods and the victims of fate. As we have seen previously, older stories do not always end so positively for the main protagonist – some are darker tales in which characters come to a sticky end.

Here in the first world, after at least three centuries of enlightened thinking and extraordinary advances in science and medicine, we are not so fatalistic. We expect our heroes to survive. We want happy endings for our characters but we want to feel that they have earned them. Although we do accept stories in which a hero fails and life turns negative, this is not the norm within fantasy fiction.

We are also a far more sophisticated and sceptical audience now. We have seen how wars, when viewed from a distance, seem ill-advised and pointless. We have seen leaders that are self-serving and governments that lie and deceive their people. Our heroes in literature reflect this more discerning approach.

THE RISE OF THE ANTI HERO

In the twentieth century, after World War I, we saw the emergence in greater numbers of the antihero. Antiheroes are not the opposite of heroes but rather those that come to heroism reluctantly and do not fit the traditional mould. They may not appear as heroes – often they are small, scrawny and underweight, more intellectual than muscular, though some are physically impressive and resourceful {Mad Max- the road warrior for example}. They are initially suspicious or solitary and unwilling to get involved. They will often defy authority and deny the company of their society. They are outsiders.

Antiheroes have been around for centuries as literary characters but last century they grew in numbers in books and film. Rhett Butler in *'Gone with the Wind'* is one such character. The hard-bitten cynical private eye Philip Marlowe in crime fiction is another literary example. He turns up in Hollywood film noirs such as *'The Big Sleep'* and *'The Maltese Falcon'* featuring Humphrey Bogart. Bogart is the epitome of the anti-hero in mid-20th century popular culture and many who come after are modelled on his persona, both in cinema and literature.

World War II and the atomic bomb made us all a little less sure of the world in which we lived and the protagonists in literature and film reflected this. By the end of the 1960s, heroes were very often characters who not only questioned authority but defied it and made their own rules to live by. They became anti-establishment as well as anti-heroes, becoming the dominant representation of the hero within our culture.

HERO AND VILLAIN

Some of the heroes within stories are equal parts villain but because of their charm or audaciousness, they win over the reader. These characters are fascinating because they are not like the conventional hero or like people we would meet in our own lives. Their wickedness has a strong appeal, so long as it doesn't offend our moral code. The vampires of Anne Rice's *'Interview with the Vampire'* are an example of this kind of protagonist.

CHARACTER FLAWS

Interesting and challenging flaws in a character humanize that character. Later we look in some depth at the choice of a hero with character flaws. The hero in *'Ladyhawke'* is an illustrative example of this. This is dealt with in greater detail in **Using Film to Explain Aspects of Novels** {See Appendix for Film info}.

THE IMPORTANCE OF BEING ORDINARY

Our heroes often begin in narratives as characters much closer to ourselves than any idealized form. They have difficult complicated lives. They can be small, frail, unsure, confused, intimidated and afraid. When characters like this move from ordinariness to a hero status, they have a much wider character arc to travel through {**see Character Arc Writer I**}. Harry Potter works because we are introduced to him, as a seemingly ordinary boy, oblivious to his own powers, history and destiny; a boy who has inexplicable things happening to him. His later discovery, that he is a wizard, is as close to wish fulfilment as any reader will get. Haven't we all wished that we were someone other than who we are, with a secret history unknown to ourselves.

When vulnerable, all-too-human characters are thrown into worlds beyond their comprehension or their innate abilities, we identify with them. When they rise to the occasion and win against all odds, we cheer for them. These tales resonate for us and offer us hope in our own lives.

CATALYST HERO

Sometimes a hero serves the purpose of creating change for a secondary character, usually a companion and ally. Often the hero is the classic resourceful and capable hero that fits the traditional mould. Because of this, the companion rises to the occasion as the hero has set the example.

But just as often, the hero is blind to some obvious truth or has a prejudice which prevents them from seeing reality and the companion must fulfil part of the quest, usually a vital part, thereby becoming the true hero of the story.

It is possible to invert the story completely and have the hero, as a hero in name only. They are inept or cowardly and once again the role falls to the companion. This is the hero as clown figure. In this, the companion obviously has the major character arc.

There are elements of clown, tragic and noble hero, in the Cervantes' character of *'Don Quixote'*.

TRAGIC HERO

Tragic heroes are those who are often in the hands of fate. They choose poorly and make decisions that we know will end disastrously. We identify with them, even when what they do is considered unacceptable.

The story then becomes about watching them fall. However, they must have some redeeming features, even if these are guilt, regret and defiance.

Macbeth is one such tragic hero. We meet him as a valiant and victorious soldier returning from the battlefield. When he is greeted and promised great things – a kingdom by the soothsaying witches, we share in his dreams. We wonder, as he does, whether he needs to do anything at all or to simply wait and allow the prophecy to take place.

We watch him as he is persuaded by his ambitious wife, to commit regicide. Slowly we experience his tragic spiral into despair and damnation, as the witches' prophecies conspire against him.

But knowing that he will surely die now, we watch as he faces that death with courage. So even in such utter failure, there are still lessons to be learnt and characters to identify with.

Part of the fascination, with such characters, is the identification we make that says, *'I am glad it is not me'*.

CHAPTER TWO

THE COMMON WORLD AND BEYOND

Story Starters
Ceremonies, Rituals and Rites of Passage
The Common World
First Glimpses/The Special World
Refusal and Acceptance

STORY STARTERS

Templates for getting going

Here are some quick ways to start thinking about the direction a Hero's Journey might take.

Universal Drives.

To be loved and understood

To survive

To succeed

To be free

To get revenge

To right wrongs

To seek self- expression

To save those we hold dearest

HERO'S INITIAL POSITION

Poor

Misunderstood

Downtrodden

Persecuted

Vilified

Laughed at

Misplaced

Unjustly accused

They draw our sympathy but we must see in them some chance for a better life.

HERO'S [HOPED FOR] FINAL POSITION

A chance for:

Love

Acceptance

Position

Wealth

Prestige

Acknowledgement

Romance

Family

In a Tragic Hero tale, the main character may gain many of these rewards only to have them slip through their fingers and for the hero {sometimes now villain} to end in failure, ignominy and death.

CEREMONIES, RITUALS AND RITES OF PASSAGE

The ritual gathering of masses and individuals for story beginnings, story changers and story endings

This section could appear both here or in Writer I. Stories often begin with ceremonies and just as often end with them.

They belong in Conventional Fiction and in Fantasy Fiction, although some rituals are more likely to appear in the latter.

We all live our lives surrounded by ceremonies signifying important temporal landmarks or significant attainments by individuals. The western traditions we recognize include:

- births
- baptisms
- birthdays and bar/bat mitzvahs
- communions
- employment and retirement
- engagements and weddings
- home ownership, housewarmings and parties
- retirements
- funerals

These are some of the markers of the progression through life. We organize awards, testimonials, graduations and the like as ways of acknowledging achievements.

We also have trial by jury, divorces, elections, political rallies, pageants, balls, dances, concerts, plays, performances, mardi gras, celebrations of social and historical significance and nationhood, religious ceremonies and gatherings.

As vehicles within story structure these ceremonies, rituals and rites of passage are very useful, since they focus an individual and a community in a very specific way. Coming of age, the unification of lovers, initiations into a tribal or social group are just some of the events that occur at significant points in story structure, usually at turning points.

Beyond our 21st century western traditions we can use the gatherings of other cultures. These might include:

- Circumcision initiations
- Crowning of Kings, Queens, chieftains, emperors and empress'.
- Sacrifices to Gods
- Executions
- Contests between rivals in the arena
- Drinking initiations
- Hallucinatory visions as communions with the Gods and/or Nature
- Individual worship/meditation
- Testing of the individual for endurance and bravery by the society
- Testing of the individual for worthiness by the society
- Trial by fire, combat or quest
- Shunning, banishment and exile
- The demonization of one group by another within a region

Because of the power inherent when numerous individuals focus as one, we can use these gatherings as story signifiers, amplifiers that give our tale great vigour and importance.

THE COMMON WORLD

The everyday and the desire to escape

Our hero will often begin their story in a common world. It is a world we are familiar with – it is the suburbs or an apartment in the city or perhaps it is a place that we are at least superficially familiar with, such as life on a farm or a boat. Even if our story begins within a medieval prison {see *Ladyhawke*} we are at least familiar with it from previous stories. **This world is normal, ordinary and pedestrian for the focal character.**

The world may be excruciatingly boring or appallingly oppressive or even physically dangerous but this is the world our hero is stuck in. And from day to day nothing much changes except possibly to get worse.

Sometimes this ordinary world is one of wealth and privilege but nonetheless they feel trapped within it and long to enter the other world. Perhaps it is our own familiar world which to them seems exotic because it offers freedom from privileged restrictions, for example *'The Prince and the Pauper'*.

In Writer I. we discussed Backstory/'What is at Stake?'/and what is the Central Theme of the story. All of these elements are linked. They create a nuanced focal character. Many of these elements become apparent in The Common World.

The backstory sets up what has happened in the past; those things that make the hero the person that they are, both negatively and positively. The backstory informs the reader of the hero's faults, compulsions and emotional and spiritual wounds, and most importantly their needs and desires. It gives a subtle explanation of the damage done and what needs to be repaired in the hero's life.

This in turn becomes part of what the hero is striving for, even if they don't know it. On the surface, it may be a golden fleece or some mythic treasure but beneath there is something more profound being sought, some restoration of the soul.

This is bound up with 'What is at Stake?' What does the hero and their companions /society stand to win if they succeed or lose if they fail.

Remember 'What is at Stake?' exists on two levels – the immediate goal of defeating the adversary on the surface but also a deeper challenge – some kind of internal need that has to be satisfied. This is because 'Conflict' – striving for the task is always linked with 'The Emotional Core', which is at the centre of the protagonist's needs.

These two – Backstory and 'What is at Stake?' focus the writer on producing the Theme - for example: the power of love to transform or the strength of friendship to prevail over all odds.

Why are they mentioned here? Because these important story elements are set up in the early part of your story – in Act One. **In Act One and in the Common World.**

For it is here that we see our focal character at their most revealing – needy, wounded and put upon. And it is most often here that others place expectations on our hero to succeed or ridicule them, believing that they will always be a failure.

It is often here that our main character makes decisions to commit, which are an extension of their internal needs, as well as the external threat. Get these elements right at the start of the story and your readership will follow you anywhere.

FIRST GLIMPSES/ THE CALL TO ADVENTURE

Something is happening here?

Often the first glimpses of the Other World appear to puzzle and intimidate the inhabitants of the Ordinary or Common World. While some heroes are willing to leave this world, for some there is an element of reluctance. Sometimes this is fear of the unknown or a sense of duty to their immediate family but for whatever reason they will deny the call of the supernatural world a number of times, often three. {See **MAGIC NUMBERS Chapter Three**}

REFUSAL AND ACCEPTANCE

Opportunity knocks but will I open the door?

Our heroes are reluctant to get involved for a multitude of reasons but find themselves caught up, sometimes against their better judgement. With some characters, an audience cannot be sure whether they will commit to the quest, until the final moment when they have a change of heart or a threat arises that provides a point of no return.

'Refusing the Call' gives an audience a pause in the narrative. In that pause, we see the fears of the hero and the concerns of those who do not want him or her to go.

We know our world to be a place that is not simply black and white but many shades of grey and our heroes reflect this within the world they live in. Their reluctance often stems from self- preservation, awareness of the falsity of the world and their own feelings of inadequacy.

Eventually circumstances will overwhelm them and they will take those first tentative steps into the darkness.

Your challenge in the ordinary world {see **Story Structure Act One WRITER I.**} is to set up why the hero wants or needs to leave. You must establish what the hero needs to learn. Often what they will learn on their quest will pay dividends back in the common world. Bravery, cunning, sophistication, wealth, fame, skill, maturity, are all rewards or forms of personal growth that will make the common world easier to deal with.

The domineering parent, an oppressive state or social system, being persecuted, hunger and poverty, the puzzle and allure of love, fear of the unknown, lack of success at a particular task – these are some of the problems that clearly need to be established within the common world.

First Glimpses of the Other World may offer a way out that is embraced willingly or it may be a way that the hero fears and is reluctant to engage with and is finally forced into the action of **Crossing the Threshold.**

Most of these challenges will be met during the quest and therefore we know, as an audience, that life will be better when the hero returns. The hero will be transformed and this of course is their character arc, their **Arc of Transformation.**

Sometimes the hero does not return to the ordinary world but remains in the supernatural world. However, what they failed at, in the common world, they will succeed at in the other, in this way the circle is completed. There are variations on the form and they represent versions of the hero's journey that defy convention and are hence more interesting.

Harry Potter does not wish to save the Common World or bring back any benefits to it. For him it is a completely loveless and oppressive place. Saving the Common World, in the end, is a by-product of his need to save the Wizarding World. He does not discover any of his quests {the smaller ones relating to each novel} or his Ultimate Quest {facing and defeating Voldemort} until he enters the Supernatural World. And it is that world's community that has expectations of him. At the completion of the saga he remains within the Supernatural World and it has become his Common World.

CHAPTER THREE
STEPPING ACROSS

Crossing the Threshold
Threshold Guardians
Magic Numbers
A Test of Character
Exercise 1
The Quest/The Special World

CROSSING THE THRESHOLD

The Point of No Return at least till the Adventure is over

The first sign that a hero has moved from the ordinary world is that they have crossed the threshold. Often this is a physical barrier. It can be entering a cave, a tunnel, a wormhole in time, stepping onto a ship, mounting a horse, joining a fellowship of like-minded adventurers or myriad other physical entrances. However willingly or reluctantly they commit to this action they know that having stepped across the threshold, they cannot turn back. Circumstances will change; they will not be as they once were. A process of growth has begun. Knowledge, skill, courage, ingenuity, cunning, compassion and camaraderie are all on the ascent.

When Luke Skywalker arrives at the frontier spaceport of Mos Eisley and enters the space cantina, he has crossed the threshold. When Harry leaves the Dursleys with Hagrid and enters Diagon Alley, he has crossed the threshold.

When Dorothy steps out of the crashed farmhouse into Munchkinland and says, 'I have a feeling we're not in Kansas anymore, Toto!' She is telling her audience that she knows she has crossed the threshold.

THRESHOLD GUARDIANS

Halt! Who goes there?

Sometimes, though not always, the threshold is guarded and though the hero may be keen to enter she is prevented. Threshold guardians have roots in both myth and theology. The guardian has a task to fulfil. The hero must prove themselves worthy to cross and begin the Quest.

Threshold guardians are more than sentries and watch-dogs. They can be holders of arcane knowledge, wielders of magical power and unforgiving of those not equipped for the task.

The threshold guardian can be the representative of the dark force and has the role of preventing all from entering. Failing that, they will message back to the villain that the hero is approaching, so that the ultimate dark force is waiting and prepared for our hero's arrival.

Some will act independently of a villain and merely be guarding their own territory; testing the mettle of our hero to see if he or she is worthy to pass through. Galadriel's meeting with Frodo in Lothlorien, in which she allows him to see into the future, is one such example.

Sometimes the hero will beguile, cajole or trick the guardian into allowing them to pass. This approach is seen as very effective; better to outwit than overpower them. Threshold Guardians that are coerced into policing a territory, under threat of punishment, may well change sides if the hero is perceived to have a reasonable chance of winning. Or, if after the Ordeal the hero meets them, they will aid them on the return journey, since the death of the villain represents liberation for them also.

Most often the Crossing of the Threshold is the first sign of a hero rising to the challenge and the first glimpse of their hero potential – a promise of things to come, maybe even their first sign of real commitment to the Quest. But not always. If the hero is a reluctant one they may have crossed over but are still overwhelmed, cynical and self-serving or wary of commitment. The commitment to the quest may be somewhere further on in the journey.

All this is part of entering the Special World and the Trials of the Road.

MAGIC NUMBERS

The Twelve Dancing Princesses meet the Nine Nazgul

Before we embark on the Quest itself we need to discuss **Magic Numbers**. Numbers have intense power within stories and recur again and again across the millennia. In fact, these numbers are so potent and yet familiar, they appear in other aspects of life.

The number seven occurs as 'the seven deadly sins', 'the seven wonders of the ancient world', the seven colours of the rainbow and 'the seven days of creation and of the week' and recurs in the seven days the Buddha sat in contemplation of his enlightenment spot, under the Bodhi Tree.

Within western literature the most famous 'seven' is the Brothers Grimm's *'Snow White and the Seven Dwarfs'* and the Seventh Seal from *'Revelations'* the apocalyptic final chapter of the *Bible*.

Other numbers of importance in European literature are nine, twelve and thirteen. Twelve is associated with disciples, dancing princesses and the Labours of Hercules. *'The Lord of the Rings'* has nine rings that ensnare the unsuspecting and nine members of the Fellowship that set off from Rivendell and are threatened by nine black riders – The Nazgul. There are nine worlds that Odin surveys in Norse Mythology.

Thirteen is often considered unlucky. This stems from various myths including the seating of disciples at the Last Supper in Christian stories and the arrival of Loki at a funeral in Norse legends.

The most common number used in stories is the number three; three pigs and bears, also three wishes and three challenges. Rumpelstiltskin appears three times to help the poor girl whose father foolishly boasted 'she could spin straw into gold'. Demanding her first- born child, he returns for three nights and each evening she attempts to guess his name, in order to save her child.

A TEST OF CHARACTER

It is in the Quest that 'three' is most significant as a test of character. The hero will make an attempt that fails twice but succeeds the third time. The hero faces the first test but fails because they have not learnt what is needed. Perhaps they have come with expectations, assumptions, pride and arrogance. They make a second attempt but keeping the same mindset they still fail. Finally, they return with an open mind and a humble heart and successfully complete the challenge.

In other versions, the hero will face three separate tasks, each one more dangerous than the last. Sometimes each challenge will call on a different skill or characteristic of the hero. Another version will have three brothers face a challenge or a foe and two will fail or choose foolishly, whilst the last, usually the youngest succeeds. The tale of *'The Deathly Hallows'* in *Harry Potter* uses this motif.

Start observing the recurrence of numbers within stories and in day to day life and note their significance for use in your own stories.

EXERCISE 1

Create a challenge or obstacle that must be passed and create three attempts, two of which fail. Create a reason or realization why the third attempt succeeds. Another variant can be that the girl doesn't fail but succeeds each time against the danger and after the third challenge has proved herself worthy and is granted a boon. Here is a beginning.

There was once a bright, young seamstress who lived with her poor widowed father on the edge of a dark wood. On All Hallows Eve a dire wolf came out of the forest in search of prey. In the moonlight, she sat with her needle and thread undisturbed by his presence. He turned to her and said ...

In your version of the confrontation between the girl and the wolf, the girl has just her needle, thread and her wits. How will she defeat her nemesis? What reward will she claim?

Remember she must be tested three times. What are the implications of a talking wolf?

THE QUEST/THE SPECIAL WORLD

Destiny calls

The Quest is the journey, challenge, adventure that will take the hero and his or her companions out of the ordinary world and into the Special World.

THE SPECIAL WORLD

Here is the chance for the author to work with mood and atmosphere. Here you will create the sensory sensations of this new and bewildering, often dangerous world. Almost immediately on leaving The Shire, the hobbits in *'The Lord of the Rings'* find themselves in danger and the presence of evil begins to close in on them. By the time they reach the 'Prancing Pony' Inn, they are aware that they are in mortal peril and being followed and it is only through 'Strider's' wise counsel that they are not murdered in their beds. {see **Creating Atmosphere W.1**} The Quest and the nature of the Special World go hand in hand.

THE QUEST

The Quest represents a chance to change aspects of character, to escape a drab existence, to live out a dream, to face and destroy an enemy that confronts the hero. For a community, it represents the chance for the hero to bring benefit to the society and change the fate of those who are threatened by calamity.

The Quest probably began within hunting communities, as the story of seeking out a kill that would feed the tribe. Over time the story of one of these kills would be told around the campfire. Perhaps there was one significant hunter who excelled or faced great danger. Each time the story was told it was embellished.

Here begins our first Hero's Journey and, as society changed and grew, our stories grew with them. Stories have always been the domain of wiser, older men and women within the tribe or community. They, who have lived a long life, weave into their stories what wisdom they have gathered over time and so stories tended to serve the purpose of both entertainment and instruction.

Over centuries the Quest would find its way from the campfire and the hearth to the market place and the royal court. Eventually those oral tales would be written down to be retold and performed. Our hero, facing the challenges of the Quest, is found in stories from every continent on earth.

The Quest stands in story lore as a test of courage, ingenuity, faith, friendship, puzzle solving and luck. The Quest takes many forms but it is always the story of a journey – physical, emotional, psychological and spiritual.

As we discussed in WRITER I. an action story must have conflict and an emotional core. **These are the building blocks of the Quest.**

Those on a quest must face trials and tribulations – the dangers of enemies, affairs of the heart, curses and carnivores. All these are all part of that Conflict.

Confusion and clarity, loss and restoration of faith, psychological terror, heartbreak, falling in love, deceit, betrayal, friendship lost and regained and physical and mental decline and restoration are the elements of the Emotional Core.

CHAPTER FOUR
MEETINGS ON THE ROAD

The Mentor
Shapeshifters
The Herald

THE MENTOR

A Guide, a gift and a push

Defeated, Humorous, Healing, Conscience – all manner of Mentors

As part of **Act 1** {See W 1. **Story Structure**} we have the **Common World** and the **Call to Adventure** and at this point we have at times the **Refusal of the Call**. Standing before our hero is the **Threshold** from which there is no turning back. Some will cross willingly and some may be forced by circumstances and some may be helped, nudged or pushed by a **Mentor**.

While some mentors are there at the start, to help ease the hero out of the Common World and into the Special World, some do not appear till later. The Hero may make the jump by themselves and the Mentor joins them on the road.

The Mentor has the role of preparing the hero for the challenges ahead. They provide knowledge and skills. They are often worldly wise and older. They offer fatherly or motherly advice and wisdom to counter youth and inexperience. Sometimes they offer up magic talismans, weapons and enigmatic riddles that the hero will solve, at the crucial moment. Often the hero needs to be trained and this may involve them dropping their ego and submitting to instruction. This is something that they may resist initially but finally come to accept the wisdom and skill of the Mentor/Master.

Obi Wan Kenobi, Yoda and Gandalf serve this purpose. Dumbledore in *'Harry Potter'* is also a Mentor.

It must be said that the Mentor / Hero relationship is the most well-known and extensively used literary device in Fantasy fiction. A little lateral thinking is needed here. You must present this relationship in new and vital ways. From Cinderella and her fairy godmother to Harry and Dumbledore your audience has known versions of this relationship all their lives. A new slant is required.

Sometimes the kind of training that the hero receives at the hands of the Mentor is subtle and experiential. The protagonist may not be aware that they are learning new skills or receiving vital information. Dumbledore plays this kind of Mentor with Harry- a kind of 'human chess' playing mentor. Mentors may not fully inform or advise their disciples. They can and do withhold knowledge from the hero, for very specific purposes. They may feel that the protagonist is not ready and the hero needs to grow before they are capable of using the knowledge.

This serves a particular function in storytelling. Like the hero we are kept in the dark and only discover the true meaning of other characters, situations and incidents as the main characters do. We become ready as the hero does. Revelations occur and things that appeared to be one thing are another. Subtle ironies are revealed and much of this can be part of the plans or precautions laid out by the Mentor.

There can be little doubt that Dumbledore has long- term plans for Harry and is allowing him to enter danger and prophesied futures as the stories develop. But for Harry, Ron and Hermione, and of course us the reader, these events are the linear occurrences that the characters go through. If there is a larger plan, we can't see it but we have the feeling that Dumbledore is playing a very long game that will use all the players. We also know that Dumbledore is making up parts of the plan, as new events, information and circumstances appear; for he too has not all the information and is searching for clues. His plan to have Harry face Voldemort is very much a work in progress.

{On this note - see **Triumvirate –Hero, Mentor and Villain Chapter Five**}

DEFEATED MENTORS

Mentors can be those heroes who travelled the same road and failed previously. They will pass on their information and advice to the new hero, in the hope that he or she will succeed. Sometimes they will not give the information required, as they do not recognise the worth or the readiness of the hero. There may be a period of trials or a significant incident that convinces the Mentor that our Hero is ready. Only then do they offer guidance and point our hero and their comrades in the right direction. Sometimes it is the love and faith of companions that convinces a Mentor of the value and true spirit of the Hero.

HUMOROUS MENTORS

There are instances when the Mentor is a joker or a wise fool, often being a sceptical commentator on the predicament of the hero, ready with a comical quip or ironic aside. At first, they may not appear as Mentors at all. Whilst they will ridicule the situation, at the crucial moment they will have vital wisdom or encouragement to offer. When this occurs, the reader knows that it is all important, as the true character of the Mentor is finally being revealed for a significant purpose.

HEALING MENTORS

These mentors have the knowledge and wisdom to restore order but they must engage the hero in this. They will supply the vision and the hero will supply the heart, mind and courage. Both Dumbledore and Gandalf are on a mission to restore order and heal the wounds of their world. Remember this is an aspect of a character not the fully fleshed out personality. They can be this and so much more.

CONSCIENCE AS MENTOR

This is a set of principles, a moral code that the hero lives by. Their mentor may have been a parent, a grandparent or a previous hero that they looked up to. There is no actual physical presence for they are often dead. The previous mentors' ideas, beliefs and actions have been internalised in our hero. The Mentor lives within and the hero will cite them as a guide, often using a piece of homespun folk wisdom, for example, *'My Grandaddy used to say…'* Sam in *'The Lord of the Rings'*, when marvelling at some fantastical place or facing the long struggle, often recites things said by his *'Old Gaffer'*.

ALL MANNER OF MENTORS

Mentors can be deep inside the hero, a constant and substantive presence or a number of minor mentors each of whom give advice and protection for part of the journey. Frodo in *'The Fellowship of the Ring'* has a series of Mentors. All his life his Uncle Bilbo has told him stories of strange far-away places, all of which has laid the foundations for his own adventures. Gandalf appears and offers advice and dire warnings and sets him on the road out of The Shire. On that road, he receives protection and guidance from Aragorn {Strider} and the royal elves Elrond and Galadriel. All these characters take on the role of Mentor to varying degrees. Even Frodo's faithful companion Sam offers insight and guidance at times, for the Mentor is a role like all the other archetypes. It is not a character itself. In his better moments, even Gollum mentors Frodo.

Sometimes Mentors will appear in Act I to urge the Hero on their way. Other times they will not appear till Act II where they will offer much needed guidance. Having guided and trained our hero, the Mentor must at some stage of the journey leave the hero to travel on alone. Alone but hopefully prepared for the final dangers that they must face without help.

Now we are in Act Two and facing all the complications that are intertwined with Conflict and the Emotional Core. At this point on the Road of Trials various archetypes appear. Some will help and some will hinder and some will threaten our Hero and company.

SHAPESHIFTERS

Beings that are not as they first appear

In their most obvious and observable form, Shapeshifters can be witches, werewolves, vampires, demons and the like. But they also take the shape of less threatening figures, which can appear mild and harmless and then transform themselves. Harder to discern are those whose emotional states shift to make them psychotic, sociopathic and murderous. The boy king Joffrey in 'Songs of Fire and Ice/Game of Thrones' is one such example. This is where the shape that has shifted is internal. The character may explode into great rages, commit acts that seem counter to the positive outcome the hero seeks or be sly, cunning and difficult to decipher. This creates great tension within the story. The twin personalities of Dr Jekyll and Mr Hyde are one obvious example, as is Count Dracula. The far more complex and initially inscrutable character of Severus Snape is another example. {see **Irony Writer 1.**} Remember that these archetypes are parts of personality but never the whole persona. In some characters, they may be so deeply embedded and so powerful as to be the greater part of whom they are. In others, they may be only one facet of a complex and multifaceted personality.

And because Shapeshifters are not as they appear, this illusory state is perplexing to both the hero and the reader. It serves to create a sense of mystery and opens up story possibilities. To not be able to put your finger on the true nature of a character or their motivations and/or trustworthiness is a great asset to story structure and development. It enlists the reader in the intrigue that follows. In stories in which the main character is male, Shapeshifters are often female and it is the emotional involvement of our hero that creates intrigue. They are lured by the romantic or sexual promise of the Shapeshifter. In crime fiction, these female Shapeshifters are often described as 'femme fatales', literally 'deadly females'.

Shape shifters are sometimes villains, sometimes aides and companions to heroes, sometimes autonomous characters along the journey.

THE HERALD

Those who announce a challenge, who set out the nature of conflict or leave dire warnings

The Herald announces a challenge or a coming battle or demands that the hero desist. The herald of a villain may well demand that the challenger returns to from whence they came or face the danger that moving forward threatens. In this respect, they are also serving as a Threshold Guardian but they will clearly set out what danger the Hero is embarking on. A positive herald may announce the nature of the challenge and have no affiliation with a villain at all.

Heralds are not necessarily flesh and bone; a dream or nightmare, a disembodied voice, a vision, a ghost all serve notice on a hero that they are entering a world about to change. The witches in *'Macbeth'* or *Hamlet's* dead father on the battlements of Castle Elsinore are heralds calling the protagonist to action. Sometimes the herald is a natural phenomenon, such as a rising tide or a gathering storm. Birds and the activities of animals and movements within the earth can all work as heralds. This is particularly evident in the early chapters of *'The Dark is Rising'* by Susan Cooper.

CHAPTER FIVE
DANGER AND DARKNESS

The Road of Trials
Tragic Heroes on the Road of Trials
Companions and Allies
All in One
The Psychology of Fear
The Villain
Master and Pupil
Triumvirate – Hero, Mentor and Villain
The Shadow
The Trickster
The Rival

THE ROAD OF TRIALS

Act Two and how our Hero is tested

Being in Act Two {See **W.1 Story Structure**} has very specific properties. Our hero must travel and grow and as this happens they will arrive at certain points in the journey. In the general scheme of things {i.e. story structure} they are plot points and of course turning points. Points where the situation changes for the better or worse, where personal challenges and decisions are made. {See **WRITER I. Turning Points**}

Naturally these turning points are the trials that the hero and companions face. And these trials will often manifest physically, within the landscape, as potent dangers. Landscape and villainous characters become entwined – almost one. Very often these will be trials that increase in power and danger. Larger stories, particularly sagas have many trials to face before the final confrontation, for example Frodo and the ever-increasing terror and addiction of the One Ring in Tolkien's trilogy. In a shorter story the number of trials is often that 'magic' number three.

As our hero travels the road they will find those who want to thwart them and those who want to aid them. Often there are a number of enemies, spies, false friends, those under the influence of evil or those in the pay of dark forces that stand in the road of our hero. Each one is a danger and a threat. Generally speaking, threats and dangers become more pronounced the closer we get to the final encounter. The Nazgul, the nine black riders who are searching for the One Ring are the advance guard of the Dark Lord. And terrifying as they are, they are only a taste of what is to come in the end.

TRAGIC HEROES ON THE ROAD OF TRIALS

A fatal error and damnation

If this is a negative story involving a Tragic Hero then somewhere, often early in the second act, they will commit a crime or a foolish act that will doom them inevitably. Now each of the trials that confront them throughout Act Two is an attempt to keep the inevitable defeat at bay.

Eventually the forces pitted against them will gain the upper hand and they will pay with their life. If the hero has companions in Act One they will gradually lose them in Act Two until they are isolated and damned. {See **Losing Your Soul/A different Kind of Ordeal Chapter Eight**}

COMPANIONS AND ALLIES

Foolish, Wise, Gifted, Humorous, Conversationalist – a coterie of Companions

Our positive hero has allies and a few will become companions, some only briefly along the road. And these come in many forms.

FOOLISH COMPANION

Some of these make mistakes that only increase the danger and the excitement {Merry and Pippin in *'The Lord of the Rings'*}. But these same clumsy fools will at certain times draw on reserves of courage and ingenuity that surprise and please the reader. Like all archetypes they can and do change within a character.

A foolish companion is changed by circumstance at some important turning point into a braver, wiser more gifted companion.

WISE OR GIFTED COMPANION

Others will have special abilities that help solve predicaments that the group face. Hermione with her logic and organisation in *'Harry Potter'* is one such example. The story that involves a fellowship of adventurers will have a number of characters who each have a special gift, a way of seeing or a piece of knowledge that will aid them in The Quest.

HUMOROUS COMPANION

Some companions offer comic relief for the dark times they progress through. Both Ron Weasley and Neville Longbottom serve this function through two thirds of the *'Potter'* saga. Notice how their names are amply suited to represent figures of fun or even ridicule {see **Character Names W.1**}. After which they take on other archetypes such as conscience mentor and hero, as the story deepens and the consequences become dire.

COMPANION AS CONVERSATIONALIST

Still others give insight or serve as a sounding board for concepts and explanations. {See **Dr Watson in 'Sherlock Holmes' Narrative Positions W.1**} Their function is to provide ideas and information in a natural conversational way. This, if done well, has a flow to it but if done badly becomes exposition. {See **The Sin of Exposition W.1**}

ALL IN ONE

Companions can be a mix of any and all of the above.

We are traveling with these companions and we will feel an affinity with each of them in turn. The companions make the journey richer by offering aspects of personality that our main character may not have or may not reveal. They will also force the hero to take on new archetypes themselves and most importantly they will question the hero's assumptions and actions.

THE PSYCHOLOGY OF FEAR

And how it relates to Fantasy Writing

As we are now in Act II and on the Road of Trials the danger quotient is rising. This seems an appropriate point at which we might look at the nature of fear and how it relates to writing a story.

Somewhere in our far distant past we invented language. Our communication developed from grunts, animal mimicry and hand signals into elaborate passages of spoken words. These had subjects and objects, actions, pauses, emphasis, beginnings and endings. All of this happened long before we formalized it in writing. Probably for several thousand years we created and used an ever increasing, ever more complex group of sound communications that consolidated as language. We used it before we began farming and settled into villages and settlements, at which point we would have begun the rudiments of writing, probably in symbol form. We can assume this because of those hunter- gatherers that have been closely observed by anthropologists, in the last two hundred years. Language, even unwritten, would have had several thousand words and we would have used it by day to help us hunt and by night to keep us company around the campfire. Here storytellers first used language to convey parables, to teach skills and most importantly to ward off the darkness.

Let us for a moment put ourselves in the place of hunters using that language during the hunt. Each man and youth would have been strung out along a line – armed and seeking to flush out prey. Since staying together in a large group would have frightened off animals, it was necessary for each hunter to hunt independently, yet close enough to call to others for aid. Here out on the grasslands of the veldt strung out along a line, you might as easily become the hunted as be the hunter. Moving through the high grass the intensity of fear would have been palpable. Jungian psychologists believe this awareness of imminent danger exists as part of our collective unconscious - something that has been passed on to each and every one of us down the millennia. Deep within our brains we have a pre-knowledge of danger, an awareness of threat; of the beast that springs unseen from the darkness. Every hunter would have known that trepidation and anticipation.

Anticipation is one of the key elements of imaginative storytelling for it is not the action but the dread of it that is most potent. This constant build to confrontation within a story, when executed with control, will make the writing irresistible. Think of the journey through the Mines of Moria in *'Fellowship of the Ring'* and the level of claustrophobic dread throughout.

{Time to read the Novella – *Of Mice and Men* by John Steinbeck}

Observe the build-up within *'Of Mice and Men'*, as we know instinctively that Lenny, with his clumsy strength and slow wits, will bring about his and George's downfall. You feel the unbearable tension as the lynch mob move in on them and George pulls out the …… { If you haven't read the story, now is the time noting how the fear and anticipation is controlled by Steinbeck}.

Look at the way the journey to Castle Dracula is built in Bram Stoker's masterpiece. The townsfolk, the less than willing guides, the sounds in the distance, the silence of the empty hall as he waits to meet the Count. The constant presence of immutable evil drips from every page of *'Dracula'*.

Whatever you write, aim for nothing less than this level of control of character, setting and mood.

THE VILLAIN

The relationship between the Hero and their adversaries

The villain is and always must be fully realized. They are not an archetype in themselves but can be made up of a number of archetypes, particularly the Shadow. They should not just be a manifestation of evil incarnate. And if they are evil incarnate and do not appear, except as the unseen puppet master, then you need to make their confederates well defined and harrowing.

A visible Villain should have backstory, some purpose, perhaps even some vulnerability. Make this character as fleshed out and physically believable as possible. The villain is probably your most important character in your storytelling. More important than the hero, I hear you ask? The answer is a definite yes!

Remember this **Cardinal Rule: THE VILLAIN DEFINES THE HERO.**

A weak villain, that either presents no real threat or has a two-dimensional purpose or a two-dimensional personality, makes the hero appear less than what they should be. The readership will ask themselves, *'What kind of hero is this, if all they have to do is defeat this weak a challenge?'*

Not all villains need to be brightly illuminated, physical characters but they must be well defined. Some villains are more presence than substance but even these leave a voluble impression on the reader. These villains remain relatively unseen – mysterious but powerful. We know them from the effect they have on others and by the menace that their lieutenants and agents represent.

The Dark Lord Sauron, of Tolkien's *'The Lord of the Rings'*, works in an almost biblical way. He is much like the concept of Satan; not seen but felt. He is always watching, tempting and working through his underlings. We know little of him except as the creator of 'the rings of enslavement' who fell in the great battle and lost the One Ring. He remains hidden but exists as a force that is always searching for it. We feel his presence and power through his agents:

The Black Riders {The Nazgul}

Grima Wormtongue

Orcs

Urakai

Saruman

Even Gollum is an unwitting agent of Sauron. Finally, there is the power of 'The One Ring' that is a physical embodiment of the Dark Lord and works his desires on others.

It is no co-incidence that J.K. Rowling also calls her villain, at times - The Dark Lord. This is one of many homages she pays to Tolkien the master.

In the coming section on 'The Shadow' there is some detail about the backstory of Voldemort and why he is such an enjoyable, fully realized villain.

MASTER AND PUPIL

A look at Tolkien and Rowling

Whilst Tolkien laid down the modern template for the epic hero's journey, it is Rowling who has fully fleshed out characters, consistent with what is expected of a contemporary novelist.

Tolkien was a folklorist and his work is designed to crystallize and celebrate a particular form of British folklore; a folklore that predates the Norman Invasion, a folklore with its roots in Teutonic myths and the great British warrior tale 'Beowulf'.

Before U.S. author Joseph Campbell showed writers the format and conventions of the Hero's journey in the mid twentieth century, in titles such as *'The Hero with a Thousand Faces'* and *'The Monomyth'*, Tolkien had already set the journey in stone, carved with ancient runes. He achieved this because he was already a historian of folk tales and mythic poetry. All those who came after followed in awe.

J.K. Rowling took that template and fused it with the conventions of the novel to create her *'Harry Potter'* saga. In its construction Rowling's work owes more to Dickens and subsequent contemporary authors than to Tolkien for *'Lord of the Rings'* has many tropes that play against modern fast paced storytelling. The fact that he would stop a story to have a character break into song or poetry for thirty stanzas is proof that he is more interested in reviving ancient forms than any attempts at novel writing.

It is educational to look at these two sagas, *'Harry Potter'* and *'The Lord of the Rings'* for their differences as well as their similarities.

TRIUMVERATE – HERO, MENTOR AND

VILLAIN

A symbiotic relationship

One of the characteristics that both sagas have in common is the relationship between hero, mentor and villain – a dangerous and chilling association between opposing forces - a deadly triumvirate.

In Tolkien's trilogy, it is apparent that Gandalf, as a mentor, is trying to guide the quest to a successful conclusion; that is the destruction of the Ring and the defeat of Sauron. There are a number of instances where he disappears for long periods in search of information, leaving the Hobbits and their companions to fend for themselves. After despatching Frodo and Sam, he is not there to meet them at 'The Prancing Pony' but sends Aragorn in his place. He does not appear again till he is at the bedside of a convalescing Frodo, in Rivendell. Gandalf is moving behind the scenes, investigating, scouting the terrain – all manner of unexplained absences designed to give him a clearer overview. He has chosen Hobbits because they came into possession of the Ring. And it has been a small and clever creature that has succeeded in keeping the Ring from the Dark Lord for eons – one of the River folk Smeagol/Gollum. Perhaps it is small creatures that might travel unseen and finally destroy the Ring and so he places great expectations not on Elves, Dwarves or Men but on Shire folk. For Elves, Dwarves and Men, particularly Men have been tempted, tricked and have failed before.

The Mentor here exists in a power-play with the hero and the villain.

Similarly, Rowling's Dumbledore moves behind the scenes, working all the component parts of the unfolding battle of wills that exist between Harry and Lord Voldemort. He builds up a narrative of young Tom Riddle for Harry and helps him to seek out vital lost memories that will explain Voldemort's desires and his past actions. He too disappears at crucial moments in the story and leaves the heroes to fend for themselves. In these grand sagas, the plans of these mentor characters appear to be inexplicable but we feel there is method behind their actions. We, like our main characters, are kept in the dark for a great deal of the time.

The aspect of personality, that both Frodo and Harry share is humility. Neither feels he is equipped for the role. They suffer doubt, are sure that they are not the hero type and feel inadequate and overwhelmed. From the Mentor's point of view, this is what makes them suitable for the task. They will choose wisely and without thoughts of power, fame or fortune. They have the best hope of not being swayed from their mission.

From an author's point of view, this humility is what makes them perfect as main characters, as they are easily identifiable to an audience and have a large character arc to travel, within the story.

THE SHADOW

The Dark Side and its' significance

The shadow is an archetype that represents the dark side of humanity. It is found in those that are villains, those who are influenced by darker forces but also those who, for a while, profoundly lose their way.

Often the rise of the Shadow archetype is a manifestation of repressed needs and desires. It can represent the denial of positive and life affirming values and the embracing of values based on power and manipulation – darker values.

Some villains are presented as being on a mission. They see themselves as having a goal that is right and true and the means will justify the ends. In their own eyes, they may see themselves as a hero. Hitler saw his purpose in life was to unify Europe under German rule and to purify the Aryan race {see **Nazi Ideology and the Hero's Journey – Appendix**}. His methods and the mythology he built around that mission were pathological and abhorrent. But he is one of the influences that informs the creation of Voldemort and his attempt at racial cleansing in the *'Harry Potter'* saga.

For an audience, there is great satisfaction in identifying with characters who feel authentic. If a character is going to display darker aspects, then we need to be able to see why this has come about. Voldemort is believable as an adult character because we meet him at the orphanage, as an eleven-year old. Here we see a vulnerable and damaged child, with a strong awareness of the difference between himself and other children. Unlike Harry, he has control of his innate powers and uses them viciously. All that remains is for him to put a name to his differences, something that he does when Dumbledore tells him that he is a wizard. But we also see pain and hurt, the need to lash out and latent sociopathic tendencies in this abandoned boy. This allows him to be a fully-fleshed out character, when we meet him as a man. His shadow aspects are clearly defined.

Darkness, the shadow aspects of a character are integral to good storytelling.

As an aside, creatures that set out to hunt and kill our heroes are not necessarily imbued with darkness, with shadow.

Crocodiles, snakes, spiders and other creatures of the night are merely carnivorous. As terrifying as they are, they are not what we are talking about.

Evil, of the kind displayed in our characters, must involve a level of choice. When Dumbledore takes Tom Riddle from the orphanage he is bound, by the conventions of wizardry, to rescue and teach him. But Dumbledore is aware, or perhaps becomes aware, that he may have brought a viper into the school. Riddle adopts a polite, charming and helpful manner and rises through the student ranks but Dumbledore is not fooled by him. At this point in his life, when he has been offered the protection of the school, Riddle chooses to use the situation to his advantage and manipulate those around him.

The darkness within Tom grows; he has made the choice to continue along the path of cruelty and domination. Later we see him as the powerful Lord Voldemort, then travel back with Harry to his origins, observing the humanity that became twisted by darkness.

Characters that are malignant are best explained by their childhood. Those who make anti-social choices are those who have something profoundly missing from their childhoods – love, acceptance, guidance, recognition, compassion and empathy. Their choices may seem counter- productive to the world at large and sometimes to themselves but we at least understand the conditioning and the compulsions behind their actions.

Aim for this kind of clarity in your shadow characters.

THE TRICKSTER

Turning things upside down

This archetype serves the purpose of upsetting the world as it appears. Positive tricksters can and do cut a hero down to size when they become conceited or misguided. They will antagonize a villain with taunts that show an audience that the villain is vulnerable. They reveal the falsity of a social order or situation. Consequently, they provide much needed humour in our storytelling. Merry and Pippin serve this purpose in *'The Lord of the Rings'* for much of the fellowship's journey. It is only when they are separated, after being abducted, that their trickster role meshes with a level of hero role. This is because they are forced now to save themselves. Loki from the Norse Myths is a trickster – one who plots against the other gods in Asgard and who often pricks their pomposity.

A Trickster can be prankish and humorous but it can be a malevolent force as well. The Trickster more often is light-hearted and wickedly playful but trickster acts can have dire ramifications. There can be tricksters with elements of The Shadow that make them very sinister indeed.

Remember these archetypes are interchangeable masks. They are aspects of personality that characters display and can and do change as the story proceeds. Remember also that they are signposts, of where our journey is at, for our hero and their companions.

THE RIVAL

Another contestant for the same goal

This as the name suggests is another protagonist {not an archetype} who travels the same path as the hero and seeks the same goal. They will have been established, as a character, early in Act One but will have far greater influence in Act Two. They will have Shadow and possibly Trickster aspects about them. Their actions don't make them an enemy but neither are they an ally. They are the rival for the romantic companion's affections. At times, they may behave unscrupulously in order to win and thereby prove themselves unworthy of the Final Reward.

CHAPTER SIX

LANDSCAPE OF THE JOURNEY

The Landscape of the Journey
Still Waters
Dark Depths
Wide Open Spaces
Inns, Saloons and Watering Holes
The Approach to the Final Ordeal
Base Camp

THE LANDSCAPE OF THE JOURNEY

There are many places along the journey that serve certain functions in the Quest, where the landscape stands as a metaphor for an aspect of the story arc or character development. {See W.1 **Turning Points/Emotional Core, Landscape as Metaphor**}

STILL WATERS

A moment of reflection and perhaps challenge

Places of momentary reprieve exist for the hero and companions to take stock. This will be where they get to know each other better, assess their chances of winning or of surviving. It can be where the Mentor or guide fills in the information blanks for them and the readership. These places are places of relative safety. This can be because they are protected by charms, such as the invisible campsite Hermione creates in the final book *'The Deathly Hallows'*. It can be a momentary lapse in the danger when the travellers can talk on horseback or around a campfire. Rivendell and Lothlorien provide both protection and good counsel for the Fellowship's travellers in *"Lord of the Rings'*.

They are places where greater understanding grows between companions, where misunderstandings are cleared up and new insights into each other are revealed.

They are places where new bonds of friendship are forged and most importantly where love grows between two of the travellers and where rivalry with a third may begin to surface.

THE DARK DEPTHS

Something is lurking in the darkness

Places of immense danger and testing are often dark and subterranean. Caves, forbidding forests, dungeons, sewers, cellars, graveyards, haunted houses, basements, catacombs, abandoned warehouses, tunnels, subway stations all signal that a hero is to be tested.

Though they are not depths, windswept mountaintops, towers or attics also provide the same atmosphere of dread. In fact, any place that by its nature feels hemmed in and claustrophobic or even unprotected and vulnerable.

WIDE OPEN SPACES

Lost in the vast emptiness

Other places that can serve to underline the fragility of the traveller can be vast and desolate spaces. These create a feeling of insignificance, when the hero moves through them, as the enormity of the distances overwhelm the human spirit. They become a metaphor for the apparent hopelessness of the enterprise. The Dead Marshes in the *'Two Towers'* of *'The Lord of the Rings'* that Frodo, Sam and Gollum travel through is one example

INNS, SALOONS AND WATERING HOLES

Accepting drinks from strangers and other dangers

Bars and taverns are places to meet comrades and guides but equally they are where the first hints of danger may appear. The hero cannot know all who are gathering here and some could be in the pay of the enemy. This may be the place where the first test takes place and the hero and his or her companions realize just how much danger they are in.

The arrival in the dead of night of the Black Riders, at the travellers' empty bedsides, in 'The Prancing Pony' proves this to the hobbits in *'The Fellowship of the Ring'*. Behaviours begin to change here and our protagonists become wary.

THE APPROACH TO THE FINAL ORDEAL

BASE CAMP

Preparing for the final assault

Just like the place part-way up a mountain, where the mountaineers prepare for the final climb, there can be a place on the journey where the travellers take stock before the final battle. There have been fights and struggles up to this point but nothing compared with what they must face now. This is a place and a moment, where we see all the fear and uncertainty fully revealed. Difficulties between fellow travellers will be exposed, rivalries for leadership or the love interest flare up and some within the company may try to sabotage the final effort.

This undermining of the enterprise can be because one vital member of the team has some deep personality flaw that prevents them from fully participating. It can also be that they are blinded by envy and cannot see why the hero has the leadership and goodwill of the company. It may be that they are another challenger for the love interest and are determined to unseat the hero.

Finally, it can be that they are a servant of the enemy and have been a double agent throughout and this is their last, or next to last chance to thwart the project.

CHAPTER SEVEN
THE FINAL ORDEAL

Psychological Challenges within the Hero
What's at Stake?
Inmost Cave/Final Ordeal
Sacrifice, Death and Rebirth
To Defeat the Seemingly Undefeatable

PSYCHOLOGICAL CHALLENGES WITHIN THE HERO

Doubts deep down inside

Since we are interested in the psychology of the hero most of all, this part of the story is about the doubts the hero has about themselves and we may have as the reader. This is the moment when he or she prove themselves and dispel the dark Shadow aspects of their own personality and grasp the positive values they will need from here on. This may be the point, or at least approaching the point, where previous heroes have fallen and this is a daunting prospect for our hero.

Here is the chance for the hero to prove themselves beyond doubt in their own mind and claim their rightful place at the helm and to rebuff all other contenders. After these difficulties are dealt with, the leader will rally the troops and begin the final ascent.

A fabulous example of this is provided in Shakespeare's Henry V, where the night before the Battle of Agincourt, outnumbered five to one, the king walks in disguise among his troops. There beside a campfire he argues tactics and the nature of leadership, with common foot soldiers. Realising the tenor of his men he prays for guidance and victory and cleanses himself of his own self-doubt.

The following morning, aware of their failing hopes, he rallies them with a stirring speech of such power that all are ready to fight beside him, in victory or defeat. This speech is called the 'The St Crispin's Day Speech'. The night before and the early morning call to arms are found in Act IV of the play and are brilliantly realized in Kenneth Branagh's film version. Looking back to Writer I this is what we have previously identified as The Emotional Core.

WHAT'S AT STAKE?

A final reminder of what is gained or lost – both externally and internally

Act IV [Scenes 18 – 67] of Henry V is an encapsulation of 'What's at Stake?' and deserves to be studied in some depth.

As I have said above, this is the moment when physically, psychologically, metaphorically and quite literally everything has come to a head and you represent it in the looks on faces, the tone of concise dialogue, the twists in the plot and the placement of characters within a poignant, metaphorical landscape.

Often in a journey our heroes may stand at a point that visually declares this idea. They might be at the base of a castle that needs to be breached. They could stand at the end of a battlefield facing an enemy, the edge of a pier or the prow of a ship, the mouth of a cave or any number of other symbolic places that illustrate their predicament. Sometimes a stirring speech is given, sometimes a great quietness falls over the company and few words are spoken. Looks are exchanged and stillness pervades. This landscape is a metaphor for all that has gone before and all that now must be faced.

But as we are writing novels here and not shooting film, you will need to convey that the company are whipped into a frenzy or quiet and overawed **in powerful words**. This is a very delicate and definitive moment of writing and will require all your skills as a storyteller.

INMOST CAVE/FINAL ORDEAL

Facing that final fear or foe

Christopher Vogel in his wonderful book *'The Writer's Journey'* identifies the last trial as the Inmost Cave, in which the hero must face the Final Ordeal. This trial which will decide the protagonist's fate must be the most threatening and frightening of all. We are descending into darkness. For here is where the climax of the story occurs and its goals are held in the balance. Here is what some writers call 'the dark night of the soul'. By now we are at the climax of Act Two {see **WRITER I. Story Structure Act 2 Chapter One**}

It is at this final confrontation point that gifts given by lovers, companions and patrons come into their own and help win the day. Among these can be wisdom, self-belief, a physical object or the power of love. There has been an emotional and physical journey for the hero and now is the moment where the hero not only faces their ultimate enemy and external terrors but also their own internal fears; they face their demons.

For Frodo in *'Lord of the Rings'* it is the final ascent of Mount Doom, where he is driven into madness by the Ring and almost completely possessed by it. Here he attempts to resist its power over him and fling it into the fire. This and the following scene are part of…

SACRIFICE, DEATH AND RESURRECTION

Back from the dead and its' primal meaning

For Harry, in *'The Deathly Hallows'*, it is where he realises that part of Voldemort's soul lies within him and he must sacrifice his own life, to defeat his enemy. In the Forbidden Forest, he stands before the Dark Lord ready to lay down his life. Harry faces his 'dark night of the soul'; his inmost cave and his ordeal, only to find after a great and tumultuous battle that, having died, he is in some form of limbo.

He meets Dumbledore in a railway station, an embarkation point, between life and death. He can choose to go on to death or return to life. In other words, he is offered resurrection. {See W.2 **Eye of the Storm Chapter Eight**}

Returning, he has one final encounter but now many things are in place. We have travelled with him on a long spiritual journey; we have watched him sacrifice his life, sure that he was going to die. We watched him choose to come back to the real world. We know that our hero is ready for the final confrontation and his enemy's hours are numbered.

This concept of death and rebirth is central to the hero's journey and is found in many myths, legends and narratives. It resonates with deeply held communal beliefs in the notion of transformation of the individual; psychically, spiritually and physically. The story, at this point, does what tribal ritual has done for centuries. It becomes a narrative form of 'rebirth' that parallels the real-life initiation ceremony.

The hero becomes lost in the whirlpool, serenaded by the sirens into ecstasy, seared by the sorcerer's flames to the point of near unconsciousness, seemingly dead and lifeless. And from here they rise again and transfigured they become, if only briefly, a demi-god able to defeat the seemingly undefeatable.

This moment in your story is what all the previous harrowing close calls have been building to. This is the major climax of your storyline and the great crescendo you have been promising for so long. We are on the cusp of Act II and Act III.

TO DEFEAT THE SEEMINGLY UNDEFEATABLE

Mustering all those writing skills for the Great Climax

Here our hero faces the confrontation that has been promised to the reader for so long – the final showdown with The Shadow Villain; a villain that oozes the darkness that has been building throughout.

In a well-conceived story, the possibilities for revelations at this moment are huge. Perhaps the enemy has always been in the company itself. Perhaps they are a member of the hero's family and the final ultimate sibling rivalry is confronted.

Perhaps too, the villain has been a Shapeshifter and their true visage is finally revealed. There are many possible variations of the villain.

Here is a moment in your writing when so many of your skills coalesce. You will be creating

- An atmospheric setting using landscape as metaphor
- Arresting and concise dialogue
- Pace and rhythm that suits the action
- Ironic twists that the audience hasn't seen coming or that one of the characters has failed to see {could be the hero or the villain} whilst we as an audience have long been aware
- Realisations and revelation
- A statement of theme, usually placed subtly in the dialogue or encapsulated in the setting/landscape that emphatically underlines what is truly at stake here
- A powerful action scene GREATER THAN ANY THAT HAS GONE BEFORE

{see W. 2 **The Climax- Various Aspects and Possibilities Next Chapter**}

Because all these are aspects of the final climax, you will need to blend a great many of your acquired skills – the ones we discussed at length in WRITER 1.

CHAPTER EIGHT
THE PSYCHOLOGY OF THE FINAL ORDEAL

Crisis of the Heart
Crisis of Personality
The Eye of the Storm
The Climax – Various Possibilities
Exercise 2
Losing Your Soul/ A Different Kind of Final Ordeal

CRISIS OF THE HEART

Will they find each other?

A crisis of the heart is often integral to the climax of a final ordeal. Whatever the physical danger, the true issue is whether the two lovers will find each other. This is played subtly but is a subtext that has been recurring throughout the story and now is realised at the point of heightened tension. Perhaps the misunderstanding that has alienated them is finally dissolved and/or the realisation of true feelings comes at this point of extreme danger and is no longer deniable. It may or may not culminate in an embrace or kiss. It may simply be implied by their combined commitment, standing side by side against the enemy.

CRISIS OF PERSONALITY

Breaking the chains that bind us

At this moment, there can be a need for the hero to change irrevocably. This often involves the destruction of forces that inhibit life and sometimes this is represented in a physical and symbolic act. The hero faces the mindset or personage that represents the hero's inability to stand on their own two feet and now they make a defiant gesture that frees them. The final ordeal can entail the destruction of a physical object – a wall or tower, a house or a prized object of the hated power figure or the smashing of an attitude that held them back.

THE EYE OF THE STORM

A moment of quiet and revelation

There is a scene, in this conflagration, which has profound meaning for the hero, companions and the story arc. It happens mid fight, reveals a profound truth and then the mayhem begins again. We have already cited one in the all-white embarkation point, where Harry meets Dumbledore, in what appears to be a spectral Kings Cross station.

It is a moment of revelation or realisation that puts things in their place.

In films, we see it in a scene where two principal characters talk whilst chaos rages around them. In novels, it might well be a thought process for our hero or a brief conversation with the adversary or a talk with their companion who makes them see the light, as they seek shelter together from the enemy's barrage.

THE CLIMAX – VARIOUS ASPECTS AND POSSIBILITIES

Aspects of the climax and their importance

We have already dealt with two of the most important elements of the final ordeal – Sacrifice, Death and Resurrection and The Eye of the Storm.

Now look at these possible elements of a Final Ordeal. Some have been dealt with before but all are included here in simplified bullet point form.

- There may be a point that the hero reaches where those who went before came to and failed. Here they may, at first, take the same approach but will see the error of their ways and have the wisdom and humility to know they are wrong and transform themselves and choose a new approach or a new path to win.
- It is at the final confrontation point that gifts given by lovers and patrons come into their own and help win the day. Among these can be wisdom, a physical object, self-belief or the power of love.
- Sometimes the Villain will escape and return in Act Three for a final battle. The Villain appears dead but is only wounded. The Hero has killed off the underlings or believes they have defeated their foe but the main danger will rise one more time.
- A crisis of the heart is often integral to the climax of a final

ordeal. Whatever the physical danger, the ultimate issue is whether the two lovers will be true to themselves and find each other.
- A female hero may find and reunite with the assertive male energy that has prevented her from being whole. A male may find that intuitive, creative energy that belongs to the female part of himself. Only when both aspects have been united does our hero succeed.
- There will be a symbolic moment where the hero faces the forces that inhibit life

- Controlling parent
    - Dystopian society
    - Life denying attitudes
    - Cruel tyrant

And at that moment of confrontation, the destruction of those negative forces can be physical but also symbolic. It may entail the possession and destruction of a physical object such as a wall, a tower, a house, the uniform the hero has been forced to wear or a prized object belonging to the hated power figure.

EXERCISE 2

Match these elements of the Final Ordeal with passages in novels and/or moments in film. This is an exercise that you will probably do over many years. Keep this set of questions close by and each time you come across one or more of these elements in a book or film then write them down.

Building up knowledge of where authors and screenwriters have used these story components is part of your role as a writer. You need to be constantly adding to your wealth of knowledge of what stories do and what writers have done.

WHERE OTHERS FAILED
1. _____
THE HERO AND THE GIFT GIVEN
2. _____
VILLAIN PLAYS DEAD TO RETURN LATER
3. _____
WILL THE LOVERS FIND EACH OTHER?
4. _____
FINDING THE OPPOSITE MALE/FEMALE ENERGY
5. _____
FACING AND DEFYING THE FATHER FIGURE
6. _____

LOSING YOUR SOUL/A DIFFERENT FINAL ORDEAL

The negative transformation

The crisis point here is not one of seeming death and resurrection but a very different outcome. In a Tragic Hero tale, this is the point at which the hero loses their soul – where they are pulled down and can no longer be redeemed.

The most literal version of this moment is in Christopher Marlowe's *'Dr Faustus'*. In this play a man of science and the magical arts sells his soul to a servant of Satan, for twenty years of magical powers. On the final night of his life he faces his quite literal 'dark night of the soul' before the denizens of hell drag him down to everlasting fire. Similarly, in *'Macbeth'* the protagonist faces the same crisis, as his enemies close in on him and the prophecies that suggested his invulnerability turn out to be elaborate deceptions.

Because Macbeth is a fallen man, from the moment he kills the King, all his trials along the road are different from those of a righteous hero. Each time he defeats his enemies he becomes more ruthless, steeped in blood and damnation. And in his final moments, he faces certain death with no hope of redemption.

If you are writing such a tragic hero tale, because this is a grand climax, you must add all the visual landscape metaphors, deep psychological insights, ironic twists, concise revealing dialogue and arresting action scenes that this negative outcome deserves.

CHAPTER NINE
WHAT IS WON AND LOST AND COMING HOME

The Ultimate Boon/ The Reward
Romantic Interlude
Self-Realization and its Aftermath
The Return Journey
Masters of Two Worlds/ Purification
And in the End...
Happily Ever Afters and their Russian counterparts

THE ULTIMATE BOON/THE REWARD

What the hero wins

Back in the positive world, we have reached the cusp of Act Two and Three – a point where the hero has defeated their nemesis and claimed what they have justly earned. Life has changed and there is celebration, recognition and sometimes a symbol of achievement – a medal of honour, a title, a position of power and respect and possibly a partner to share life with.

Joseph Campbell calls it the Ultimate Boon, while Christopher Vogler calls it The Reward. It is the pay off at the end of the adventure. This reward comes in many forms. It may be the winning of a mate, a life partner. It may be fame, fortune, replacing the tormentor with the hero who is now in a position of power and benevolence.

It may be a gift that returns prosperity to the community; that gift can be in the form of a magical talisman, or acquired knowledge or a blessing from the 'Gods' that ends the drought, the famine, the pestilence, the curse and brings prosperity and peace. Those who have treated the hero badly or dismissed him or her as a lightweight now have a new-found respect for them.

In longer sagas, the reward may appear at the conclusion of one section but is the key to new adventures. For example, the hero may have acquired a sword, a map, a protective amulet that will serve them in later ordeals. At this point their Mentor or their companions/allies may urge them on to new adventures. Or there may just simply be unfinished business to be dealt with in other lands.

ROMANTIC INTERLUDE

Love, lust and sacred marriage

It is at this point that promises of love, faithfulness, sexual encounter are given as part of the hero's new found status. Sometimes this is suggested by something as subtle as a walk between the two parties or it might be a dance that signifies a newly created bond between them.

If a larger statement is required then we are looking at the 'Sacred Marriage'- a powerful bonding that symbolizes many things for Hero, Bride/Groom and Society. It can be the ending of hostilities of two warring parties signified by the joining of a bride from one and a groom from the other. The marriage will represent new found prosperity for all and on a holistic level it implies that the natural order has been restored.

SELF REALIZATION AND ITS AFTERMATH

What has been transformed inside

For some heroes, the reward that comes at the end of The Ordeal is not physical but is spiritual, a sense of inner peace, a level of acceptance. The result of The Ordeal is that they have stopped resisting their true self or the natural order and are now in harmony with existence.

For others who have created discord, pain and possibly death and destruction, there can be a realization that they must make amends and choose another path. For some villainous characters this is the moment of atonement.

Kate Forsyth's *'Bitter Greens'* features a number of self-realizations that illustrate these ideas. Time to read this exquisite book as much of what follows involves observations of the text.

For Charlotte-Rose de la Force there is a moment of self-realization when she accepts the reality of her existence and embraces her true calling.

For La Bella Strega, in her new role, she makes amends. These insights happen close to the end of the story. The self-realization these two characters exhibit at the conclusion of the book is centred on acceptance and repentance respectively. Profound realisations are often found after the Final Ordeal and within Act III.

THE RETURN JOURNEY

On the way home or further on

Having defeated the enemy and met the challenge, seized the reward and claimed their rightful place, our protagonists begin the return journey. Sometimes this is in the direction of home where they will arrive as all conquering heroes, bringing great benefit to their society.

Or they travel on to more adventures, as they are forever changed by the experience and can never return home. All that they once loved is gone or they have changed so profoundly inside, that they can never be at one with their previous life. These kinds of figures become lone travellers – sometimes tragically heroic figures who wander the wasteland. Mad Max from *'The Road Warrior'* series and The Doctor from *'Dr Who'* are examples of this.

The return home or the travel onwards can be a time of reflection. It can be a time to take stock of where we are headed next both physically and psychologically. It is here we examine what we have learnt and what we have achieved. If this is part of a series, it is where we state where we are going to.

There are many loose ends that need to be tied up here, for we are in Act Three. [**See W.1 Act Three**]

The road back can still be paved with dangers. In fact, forces can still be unleashed that our heroes are only a few steps ahead off. There can be further adventures and a chase to the finish line. There are often examples of this in Hollywood film, where the chief danger has been subdued and is apparently dead. There is a brief interlude after which the danger springs up from where it has been lying in wait. The hero must make one final fight of it and put the menace to death once and for all. In some stories, having defeated the danger, the creature's mate comes seeking revenge.

In others, some new, unforeseen threat arises, although this is rarer it does happen. In *'The Lord of the Rings – 'The Return of the King'* the Hobbits return to The Shire to find that Saruman, in a new disguise, is terrorizing the inhabitants of Hobbiton. Together they drive him and his standover men out. This is something that their kinsfolk are unable to do but - having returned from The Quest - Frodo, Sam, Merry and Pippin are made of sterner stuff.

They are.....

MASTERS OF TWO WORLDS / PURIFICATION

To the Victor the Spoils/Decommissioning the return soldier

When our heroes return from the Special World they have mastered, the Ordinary World presents little in the way of threat or challenge. So, as Joseph Campbell describes them, they are now masters of two worlds.

Sometimes they must face one last challenge in order to be 'deblooded'- to be decommissioned, to allow them to leave behind the violence of the Special World and live peacefully in the Common World. A kind of purification occurs for them, a kind of baptism that renews them in the eyes of their society. Usually something physical happens and the body and mind of our heroes are purified. Perhaps a rival from the Common World will challenge them for ascendancy but having faced the Road of Trials they are more than a match for this contender.

Description, metaphors, thoughts, concise dialogue, landscape, rhythm and pace all come into play here.

Perhaps the hero will physically die in the Final Ordeal and then be resurrected in the hearts and minds of those he or she died for. The death is the purification and the memories held become the resurrection.

AND IN THE END......

Happy Ever Afters and their Russian counterparts

We cannot escape the question of how we want to end our stories both as a writer and a reader.

Closed ended stories end with a level of pleasing resolution-

Lovers find each other.

Prosperity returns to the community.

Villains are defeated.

Warriors and adventurers return as glorified heroes.

This kind of completion is a closed circle – a situation where all or almost all is right with the world.

There is a place for this. Happy endings work because we desire them, aspire to them and because sometimes we believe we see them in the lives of others. We know of happily married couples, fathers and mothers who love their children. The world is full of people who do noble, self-sacrificing acts with no thought of recompense or recognition; people who love unconditionally and find it in return.

But some see this kind of ending as unrealistic, unsophisticated even downright dishonest – a little too Hollywood, a little too 'Happily Ever After'. They argue that less optimistic, more open-ended approaches create stories grounded in true reality. For them the story is far more 'Russian', more like a Chekov play, much darker, less sure – with many more questions hanging over the participants. Story possibilities that leave your reader wondering and discussing are abundant in this approach.

Sometimes we can have a mix of the two, where some of our characters find peace and happiness while others must move on still searching for what they have not attained. *'Bitter Greens'* has both kinds of conclusions woven into its multi strand endings.

CHAPTER TEN
DEEPER INSIGHTS

The Character Arc as the Hero's Journey
Towering Possibilities – The Rapunzel Story
Exercise 3
Exercise 4
Exercise 5
Using Film to Explain Aspects of Novels
Exercise 6
The Hero in *LADYHAWKE* – a case study of reluctant heroes
Character Arcs
Character Flaws illustrated
Oh and Another Thing
Postface
Theory, Process, Examples, Exercises – The Age Old Method
What You Should Do Next
And Lastly....Form not Formula

THE CHARACTER ARC AS THE HERO'S JOURNEY

The symbiotic meeting of Writer 1 and Writer 2

As we know from WRITER 1 the character arc is both the physical dangers faced but just as importantly the emotional growth, the learning process our hero goes through over the course of the entire story; from ignorance, fear and inability to knowledge, courage and mastery {at least in most cases}.

The Character Arc parallels the Hero's Journey.

For a thorough and easily understood visual representation of this process, you cannot go past Christopher Vogler's 'The Writer's Journey' Stage Eleven – 'The Resurrection'. Here in step by step format you can see the journey and the arc. It is further illustrated by a cycle separated into three acts {see **Writer 1 Story Structure**}

My version below relates horizontally to the Three Act Structure but vertically above and below the line to Conflict and The Emotional Core.

HERO'S EMOTIONAL CONFLICT

*This is a simplification of The Hero's Journey and represents a traditional linear story line with positive outcomes.

ACT I

Emotional	Conflict
Persecuted/Misunderstood Unrequited/Frustrated	Displaced within the Common World
Puzzlement/Fear	First Glimpses
Denial/Concerns/Fear Reluctance	Refusal of the Call (possible arrival of Companion/Allies/Mentors)
(Optional) Possible Commitment Determination/Sense of Injustice	Initial Incident/Revelation

ACT II

Emotional	Conflict
Commitment (at least partially)	Crossing the Threshold
Growing sense of Wonder/ Growing sense of Dread/Fear	The Quest/The Special World (meetings with Archetypes including shapeshifters/shadows/mentors)
A deepening sense of commitment	1st Trial - Danger/Threat
Growing concern/ Commitment/Confidence	Enemies/Carnivores/ Testing of hero's abilities
Possible Reactions Confusion/Loss of faith/heartbreak/deceit/betrayal/ friendship lost/ physical and mental decline *Realization of what is truly at stake	2nd Trial - Stronger and more hazardous danger both physical and psychological
Total Commitment Clarity/Restoration of Faith/Love restored/ Truth realized/Friendship regained/ Physical and mental restoration	3rd Trial - Final Ordeal/Confrontation

ACT III

Emotional	Conflict
Exultation/Euphoria/Romantic and/or sexual commitment/Recognition/ Glory/ Realization and understanding	Victory and Mastery
Purification and Transcendence	Return home or further on/ Reunification

TOWERING POSSIBILITIES – THE STORY OF RAPUNZEL

A Case Study of Story Potential from the 'Tale of the Girl in the Tower'

Suppose we want to take a folktale and tease it out into a larger story, an adult story, a story that involves murder, kidnapping, sorcery, sexuality and love. Let us look at a well-known folktale and see what possibilities we can make, as novelists, out of the story. Let us pretend for a moment that we are as clever and well researched as Kate Forsyth in *'Bitter Greens'*, whose text we reference here.

Rapunzel – collected by Jacob and Wilhelm Grimm

There was once a man and a woman who had long in vain wished for a child. At length, it seemed God was about to grant their desire.

These people had a little window at the back of their house from which a splendid garden could be seen, which was full of the most beautiful flowers and herbs. It was, however, surrounded by a high wall, and no one dared to go into it because it belonged to an enchantress who had great power and was dreaded by all the world. One day the woman was standing by this window and looking down into the garden, when she saw a bed which was planted with the most beautiful rampion {sometimes called rapunzium}, and it looked so fresh and green that she longed for it, she quite pined away, and began to look pale and miserable.

Then her husband was alarmed and asked; 'What ails you, dear wife?'

'Ah,' she replied, 'If I can't eat some of the rampion which is in the garden behind our house, I shall die.'

The man, who loved her, thought: 'Sooner than let my wife die, bring some rampion yourself, let it cost what it will.'

At twilight, he clambered down over the wall into the garden of the enchantress, hastily clutched a handful of rampion and took it to his wife. She at once made herself a salad of it, and ate it greedily. It tasted so good to her – so very good – that the next day she longed for it three times as much as before. If he was to have any rest, her husband must once more descend into the garden, in the gloom of evening therefore, he let himself down again; but when he had clambered down the wall he was terribly afraid, for he saw the enchantress standing before him.

'How can you dare,' said she, fixing him with an angry look, descend into my garden and steal rampion like a thief? You shall suffer for it!'

'Ah', answered he, 'let mercy take the place of justice. I only made up my mind to do it out of necessity. My wife saw your rampion from the window, and felt such a longing for it that she would have died if she had not got some to eat.'

Then the enchantress allowed her anger to be softened and said to him: 'If the case be as you say, I will allow you to take away with you as much rampion as you will, only I make one condition: you must give me the child which your wife will bring into the world; it shall be well treated, and I will care for it like a mother.'

The man in terror consented to everything, and when the woman was brought to bed, the enchantress appeared at once, gave the child the name of Rapunzel and took it away with her.

Rapunzel grew into the most beautiful child under the sun. When she was twelve years old, the enchantress shut her in a tower, which lay in a forest. It had neither stairs nor door, but quite at the top was a little window. When the enchantress wanted to go in, she placed herself beneath it and cried: 'Rapunzel, Rapunzel, let down your hair to me.'

Rapunzel had magnificent long hair, fine as spun gold, and when she heard the voice of the enchantress she fastened her braided tresses, wound them round one of the hooks of the window above, and let the hair fall twenty metres down, whereupon the enchantress climbed up by it

After a year or two, it came to pass that the king's son rode through the forest and passed by the tower. Coming from it he heard a song, which was so charming that he stood still and listened. This was Rapunzel, who in her solitude passed her time in letting her sweet voice resound. The King's son wanted to climb up to her, and looked for the door of the tower but none was to be found. He rode home, but the singing had so deeply touched his heart that every day he went into the forest and listened to it. Once, when he was thus standing behind a tree, he saw that the enchantress came there, and he heard how she cried: 'Rapunzel, Rapunzel, let down your hair to me.' Then Rapunzel let down the braids of her hair, and the enchantress climbed up to her.

'If that is the ladder by which one mounts, I too will try my fortune', said he, and the next day when it began to grow dark, he went to the tower and cried:

'Rapunzel, Rapunzel, let down your hair to me.' Immediately the hair fell down and the king's son climbed up.

At first Rapunzel was terribly frightened when a man, such as her eyes had never yet beheld, came to her; but the king's son began to talk to her quite like a friend, and told her that his heart had been so stirred that it had let him have no rest, and he had been determined to see her.

Then Rapunzel lost her fear, and when he asked her if she would take him for her husband, and she saw that he was young and handsome, she did not hesitate; she thought: 'He will love me more than old Dame Gothel does'; and she said yes, and laid her hand in his. She said:' I will willingly go away with you but I do not know how to get down. Bring with you a skein of silk every time that you come, and I will weave a ladder with it, and when that is ready I will descend, and you will take me away on your horse.' They agreed that until that time he should come to her every evening, for the old woman came by day.

The enchantress remarked nothing of this, until one day Rapunzel thoughtlessly said to her: 'Tell me, Dame Gothel, how it happens that you are so much heavier for me to draw up than the king's son – he is with me in a moment.'

'Ah! You wicked child', cried the enchantress. 'What do I hear you say? I thought that I had separated you from all the world, and yet you have deceived me!'.

In her anger, she clutched Rapunzel's beautiful tresses, wrapped them twice round her left hand, seized a pair of scissors with the right, and snip, snap, they were cut off, and the lovely braids lay on the ground. And she was so pitiless that she banished poor Rapunzel to a desert where she had to live in great grief and misery.

On the same day that she cast out Rapunzel, however, the enchantress fastened the braids of hair which she had cut off to the hook of the window, and when the king's son came and cried: 'Rapunzel, Rapunzel, let down your hair to me', she let the hair down.

The king's son ascended, but instead of finding his dearest Rapunzel; he found the enchantress, who gazed at him with wicked and venomous looks.

'Aha!' she cried mockingly, 'you would fetch your dearest, but the beautiful bird sits no longer singing in the nest: the cat has got it, and will scratch out your eyes as well. Rapunzel is lost to you; you will never see her again'.

The king's son was beside himself with pain, and in his despair, he leapt down from the tower. He escaped with his life, but the thorns into which he fell pierced his eyes. Then he wandered quite blind about the forest, ate nothing but roots and berries, and did naught but lament and weep over the loss of his dearest wife. Thus, he roamed about in misery for some *years, and at length came to the desert where Rapunzel, with the twins to which she had given birth, a boy and a girl, lived in wretchedness.*

He heard a voice, and it seemed so familiar to him that he went towards it, and when he approached, Rapunzel knew him and fell on his neck and wept. Two of her tears wetted his eyes and they grew clear again, and he could see with them as before. He led her to his kingdom where he was joyfully received, and they lived for a long time afterwards, happy and contented.

Some Writer's Questions to consider -

EXERCISE 3

Initial Questions

How many characters do we have here?

Who is the most important character? Why do you see this person as the focal character?

Can we tell stories about each of them?

If we do, will it change who the focal character is?

WHAT IFS/WHOS/ WHYS/ BACKSTORIES
Further Questions using the approaches above.

What is the real name of the girl in the Tower?

Who names the child Rapunzel and why rename her?

Why is she in the Tower? What if there is some reason that she is placed there when she becomes twelve?

Who put her there and what is the purpose of keeping her imprisoned?

Why would the mother give up her child to this woman?

What is the girl in the Tower's backstory?

What age is she when she meets the Prince?

Is this important or can we make it important?

What is the Enchantress' backstory?

What if it is significant that she is called an enchantress and not a witch? What does that imply?

What is the Wife/Mother's backstory?

What is the Husband/Father's backstory?

We will stop here because we have gleaned some basic information from a straightforward folktale of only a few pages, asking questions that expand on the story's possibilities.

From this point on the questions are specific to Kate Forsyth's brilliant reworking of the tale. 'Bitter Greens' is an amazing adaption and an extraordinary extrapolation.

RESEARCH

ONE MORE QUESTION TO THINK ABOUT!

EXERCISE 4

QUESTION – WHAT WAS THE SOURCE OF THIS STORY IN FRENCH?

Let's look at the research behind this tale. In the preface to the book 'Bitter Greens' the author Kate Forsyth describes some of the history of 'Rapunzel'

The story is most well known as the Brothers Grimm retelling, supplied here, but there is an Italian and a French version. The French version was created by Charlotte-Rose de la Force, a high-born woman banished from the court of the Sun King Louis XIV and *"locked away in a nunnery as punishment for her scandalous life."*

She is responsible for creating the ending, in which Rapunzel's tears restore the sight of her love. This ending is reiterated in the Grimm's version but was not there in the original Italian version. Her version appears sixty-four years after the first known version, the Italian one. But here is the puzzling thing. It was not translated out of Italian till after Madame de la Force's death and she never travelled to Italy nor could she speak Italian.

So how did she get to hear this story?

What is the story potential here?

THE ANSWER TO EXERCISE 4. QUESTION SUPPLIED BELOW AFTER NEXT EXERCISE.

Having read the book, by this time, you will know the answers to all the questions asked but more importantly you will see the questions Kate Forsyth asked to create the novel.

EXERCISE 5

Answer these questions about the Story Potential of **RAPUNZEL. My observations follow straight after.**

Can we get any of these characters to intersect in the backstory? What if meetings between them in the past have direct bearing on what is happening now in Rapunzel?

What if we take those backstories of various characters and foreground them, making them fully fleshed out lives of their own?

What if the girl in the Tower is not the first?

If so, where are the rest of them?

If there are others how and when did they die? And Why?

Where did the girl in the Tower learn to sing so beautifully?

Who is the Prince and how does he come to be there in the first place?

What obstacles will be written into the story to make it difficult for her to escape?

Why can't he help her escape the first time he comes to the tower and does this serve a purpose in the novel?

Are there anymore characters that could be in this story beyond the tale itself?

What if we create a character that is not there in the Tale but has a direct connection – a storyteller?

Is there a visual metaphor that will run through the story and that shows us a way of structuring our retelling?

All these ideas are potential story elements built into this folktale. They are there waiting to be expanded upon.

My answers to EXERCISE 5.

My answers to these questions a writer might ask when looking at story potential. I suspect these are some of the questions and answers Kate Forsyth would have found when looking at Rapunzel.

Can we get any of these characters to intersect in the backstory? What if meetings between them in the past have direct bearing on what is happening now in 'Rapunzel'?

ANSWER- Yes, the mother has great potential since the longing for a child is a powerful story element? Perhaps the desire for a family can be wound up with the enchantress before the appetite for rampion, which is where the folktale begins.

The enchantress also has the potential for a larger story which can relate to her need to kidnap and imprison children.

What if we take those backstories of various characters and foreground them, making them fully fleshed out lives of their own?

ANSWER – Obviously, the child is going to forget the family she had if she was taken as a babe but if she was taken at an agreed upon time, later in her childhood, then her relationship with her parents can be foregrounded. So, we have the child, the mother and father and the enchantress each with their own life stories.

What if the girl in the Tower is not the first?

ANSWER – If she is not the first then that makes this a long term obsession and obviously a very dark enterprise.

If so, where are the rest of them?

ANSWER – They of course must be dead. But for what purpose does she use them. As she is an enchantress, there deaths must have some direct relationship with sorcery.

If there were others how and when did they die? And Why?

ANSWER – The how is unknown but each appears to have died after growing from a child to an adolescent or young woman. As to why? Again, we are looking at a spell and so we begin to conjecture for what? Here we look at what a woman might want beyond motherhood. Ageless beauty is the likely possibility.

Where did the girl in the Tower learn to sing so beautifully?

ANSWER – Here we can give her a life of her own. If she had arrived at the tower as an infant then we have the enchantress playing mother and taking care of her. This is possibly too much emotional commitment for the enchantress and flies in the face of a serial kidnapper. We need Rapunzel to arrive at a point where she can take care of herself and those intervening years explain her singing prowess and the songs she sings.

Who is the Prince and how does he come to be there in the first place?

ANSWER – This is a tale of women primarily and the men are less central but obviously he needs to come enough times for her to fall pregnant as she bears twins later. We have him coming and going on an enterprise of his own.

What obstacles will be written into the story to make it difficult for her to escape and does this serve a purpose in the novel?

ANSWER – He needs to come back several times since we need a courtship, sexual intimacy and a pregnancy. She cannot leave easily. The woven ladder is a bit flimsy as a story device and doesn't have any story dynamics to it. Loyalty to the Enchantress is unlikely, so fear is the operating force - an enchantment of some kind perhaps. As for a purpose in the novel – we are talking of the awakening of a young girl to womanhood. Desire, sexuality, pregnancy and childbirth are themes that exist throughout the tale - for the mother at the start and for Rapunzel at the end.

Are there anymore characters that could be in this story beyond the tale itself?

ANSWER – Certainly not as the original story appears but there are possibilities to expand. We are looking at stories within stories. See next answer.

What if we create a character that is not there in the Tale but has a direct connection – a storyteller?

ANSWER – The story of Charlotte- Rose de la Force as the storyteller and her imprisonment gives us an overarching structure, within which to tell the stories of the characters in *'Rapunzel'*. It becomes stories within stories and begins with the central premise 'What if *'Rapunzel'* was based on real characters in a larger story.

Is there a visual metaphor that will run through the story and that shows us a way of structuring our retelling?

ANSWER – The braiding of Rapunzel's hair and that of the girls who came before is a wonderful metaphor, for interweaving the stories of all the characters.

What is truly wonderful is the surprise twist that is at the end when the original storyteller and the source of the tale reveals herself. AND THAT ANSWER IS NEXT,

ANSWER TO EXERCISE 4. RESEARCH FROM ABOVE

But here is the puzzling thing. It was not translated out of Italian till after Madame de la Force's death and she never travelled to Italy nor could she speak Italian.

So how did she get to hear this story?

The answer is, of course, that she needs to have been told the story by someone who spoke both Italian and French and that Charlotte Rose did her own transcription and reworking.

What if we weave this mystery into the novel creating not just a folktale but a storyteller or two to tell it?

This is inspired creative thinking. She answers the question of how Charlotte-Rose heard the story by creating someone who spoke both languages but she went one step further and said -

What if I make this narrator one of the principal characters in the original story and elaborate on her backstory? [No we will not identify her in case you still have not read the book] This is what great writers do!!!

USING FILM TO EXPLAIN ASPECTS OF NOVELS

We utilize a great little film to illustrate concepts

One of the simplest and the most structurally sound of the Hero's Journey exemplars is '*Ladyhawke*' a film directed by Richard Donner.

While it is not the most well known in the genre, it is clever and atmospheric and most importantly it covers aspects of the hero's journey in an easily recognized manner. And the structures within its screenplay are very similar to those found within a novel.

It is at this point that readers should download and watch this film. Much of what we explore after this and what we have covered up to now will make more sense if you have seen the film.

Following are two film synopses – the first is simply a rundown of the characters and events. The second is broken into various sub-headings. Those relating to Writer I - including story structure and those that relate to aspects of Fantasy Fiction and the Hero's Journey found in Writer II.

Film Synopsis 1.

LADYHAWKE Writer Edward Khmara/Director Richard Donner

EXERCISE 6

Find the Three Acts/the Turning Points/ The aspects of the Hero's Journey/ the Archetypes and anything else I have covered in either half of the book. The answers are in Synopsis 2. Try not to look at them before completing this exercise.

Plot: In twelfth century Europe, **Philippe Gaston,** *"The Mouse", is a thief facing the hangman, who escapes the dungeons of Aquila, via the sewers, and flees to the countryside.* **The Bishop of Aquila** *sends his* **Captain of the Guard Marquet** *to hunt down Philippe; he and his soldiers corner the boy. Ready to execute him on the spot, they are prevented by a mysterious black knight who reveals himself to be their* **former Captain, Etienne of Navarre** *[called Navarre in the film], traveling with a beautiful and devoted hawk. Philippe tries to escape him also but whilst fleeing is scooped up by the knight on horseback and they ride off together. Marquet warns the* **Bishop** *of Navarre's return, and the Bishop summons* **Cezar the wolf trapper** *to hunt down Navarre.*

Navarre tells Philippe why he saved him: he needs Philippe's unique knowledge to lead him inside Aquila to kill the Bishop. As they travel Philippe becomes aware of mysterious events surrounding them, including the appearance at night of a black wolf and a beautiful woman, who is unafraid of the wolf.

Navarre and the hawk are wounded in another encounter with the Bishop's men; Navarre sends the hawk with Philippe to **the old monk Imperius***, to heal her. At a ruined castle Philippe finally realizes the truth, which Imperius confirms: the hawk is a woman named* **Isabeau d'Anjou***, who came to live in Aquila after her father the* **Count of Anjou** *died. All who saw her fell in love with her, including the Bishop. But Isabeau was already in love with Etienne, with whom she secretly exchanged vows.*

Accidentally betrayed by their confessor, Imperius, they flee. In his insane jealousy, the Bishop makes a demonic pact to ensure they will be "Always together; eternally apart" By day Isabeau becomes a hawk; by night Navarre becomes a wolf. Neither has any memory of their half-life in animal form; only at dusk and dawn of each day can they see each other in human form for one fleeting moment, but can never touch.

The Bishop's men arrive at Imperius' broken down fortress determined to capture Isabeau. Philippe helps her to flee to the top of the battlements where there is no escape. She accidently falls. Philippe clings to her, as she slips threw his fingers but miraculously transforms into the hawk, with the first rays of the morning sun. Philippe faces death at the hands of the Bishop's men but is saved by Navarre, now back in human form.

Navarre plans to kill the Bishop or die in the attempt, making the curse irrevocable. But Imperius has discovered a way to break the curse.

In three days, there will be "a day without a night and a night without a day": when the lovers can stand together in human form before the Bishop and the curse will be broken. Imperius travels with the threesome toward the castle and manages to persuade Isabeau of his plan to break the curse. When Philippe saves Navarre in the form of the wolf from a frozen river, Navarre is humbled and places himself in the hands of Isabeau, Imperius and Philippe. Together they enter Aquila at night, Navarre as the wolf inside a cage.

The following morning, Navarre, consumed with hatred fails to listen to Imperius. It is the third day and whatever Imperius had believed has not come to pass as they all find themselves inside the citadel, where the knight prepares to slay the Bishop. He leaves instructions to kill the hawk if he fails- the sign that he has failed will be the ringing of the church bells.

Philippe must climb back into the cathedral via the sewers and there surrounded by soldiers, he will open the doors of the Cathedral to allow Navarre to enter. But as Navarre faces the Bishop, the sky darkens through a broken skylight and we see the beginnings of an eclipse. "A day without a night and a night without a day" – at last Navarre understands Imperius' meaning. The bells of the cathedral are accidently rung and Navarre believes Isabeau is dead - put to death, as the hawk, on his instructions. Just as he is about to slay the Bishop she appears in human form; the curse has been broken as they both stand before the Bishop as man and woman.

Filled with jealousy the Bishop attempts to slay Isabeau but Navarre pins him to the wall with his sword.

The lovers and friends reunite at the doors of the cathedral, rejoicing in their good fortune.

Film Synopsis 2

LADYHAWKE Writer Edward Khmara/Director Richard Donner

Act One

The Common World

In twelfth century Europe, **Philippe Gaston, "The Mouse"**, *is a thief* [**The Trickster**] *facing the hangman, who escapes the dungeons of Aquila, via the sewers, and flees to the countryside.* **The Bishop of Aquila** *sends his* **Captain of the Guard Marquet** *to hunt down Philippe; he and his soldiers corner the boy. Ready to execute him on the spot, they are prevented by a mysterious black knight who reveals himself to be their* **former Captain, Etienne of Navarre** {*called Navarre in the film*}, *traveling with a beautiful and devoted hawk. Philippe tries to escape him* [**Refusal of the Call**] *also but whilst fleeing is scooped up by the knight on horseback and they ride off together* [**Crossing the Threshold**]. *Marquet warns the* **Bishop** *of Navarre's return, and the Bishop summons* **Cezar the wolf trapper** [*both Shadow figures*] *to hunt down Navarre.*

Act Two

Navarre tells Philippe why he saved him: he needs Philippe's unique knowledge to lead him inside Aquila to kill the Bishop [**The Quest**].

The Special World

As they travel Philippe becomes aware of mysterious events surrounding them, including the appearance at night of a black wolf and a beautiful woman, who is unafraid of the wolf [**Shapeshifters**].

Navarre and the hawk are wounded in another encounter with the Bishop's men; Navarre sends the hawk with Philippe to **the old monk Imperius** [**Mentor**], to heal her. At a ruined castle Philippe finally realizes the truth, which Imperius confirms: the hawk is a woman named **Isabeau d'Anjou**, who came to live in Aquila after her father the **Count of Anjou** died. All who saw her fell in love with her, including the Bishop. But Isabeau was already in love with Etienne, with whom she secretly exchanged vows.

Accidentally betrayed by their confessor, Imperius, they flee. In his insane jealousy, the Bishop [**Shadow**] makes a demonic pact to ensure they will be "Always together; eternally apart". By day Isabeau becomes a hawk; by night Navarre becomes a wolf [**Shapeshifters**]. Neither has any memory of their half-life in animal form; only at dusk and dawn of each day can they see each other in human form for one fleeting moment, but can never touch.

First Trial.

*The Bishop's men arrive at Imperius' broken down fortress determined to capture Isabeau. Philippe helps her [**Accepting the Quest**] to flee to the top of the battlements where there is no escape. She accidently falls. Philippe clings to her, as she slips threw his fingers but miraculously transforms into the hawk, with the first rays of the morning sun. Philippe [**Hero**] faces death at the hands of the Bishop's men but is saved by Navarre, now back in human form.*

Navarre plans to kill the Bishop or die in the attempt, making the curse irrevocable. But Imperius has discovered a way to break the curse.

*In three days [**Magic Numbers/The Ticking Clock**], there will be "a day without a night and a night without a day": when the lovers can stand together in human form before the Bishop and the curse will be broken. Imperius travels with the threesome toward the castle and manages to persuade Isabeau of his plan to break the curse.*

Second Trial

When Philippe saves Navarre in the form of the wolf from a frozen river, Navarre is humbled and places himself in the hands of Isabeau, Imperius and Philippe. Together they enter Aquila at night, Navarre as the wolf inside a cage.

Act Three

The following morning, Navarre, consumed with hatred fails to listen to Imperius. It is the third day and whatever Imperius had believed has not come to pass, as they all find themselves inside the citadel, where the knight prepares to slay the Bishop. He leaves instructions to kill the hawk if he fails- the sign that he has failed will be the ringing of the church bells.

Third Trial

Phillipe must climb back into the cathedral via the sewers and there surrounded by soldiers, he will open the doors of the Cathedral to allow Navarre to enter. But as Navarre faces the Bishop, the sky darkens through a broken skylight and we see the beginnings of an eclipse. "A day without a night and a night without a day" – at last Navarre understands Imperius' meaning. The bells of the cathedral are accidently rung and Navarre believes Isabeau is dead - put to death, as the hawk, on his instructions. Just as he is about to slay the Bishop she appears in human form; the curse has been broken as they both stand before the Bishop as man and woman.

Filled with jealousy the Bishop attempts to slay Isabeau but Navarre pins him to the wall with his sword.

*The lovers and friends reunite [**The Reward**] at the doors of the cathedral.*

THE HERO IN LADYHAWKE

A study in reluctant heroes The Mouse that roared

CHARACTER ARCS

There are many journeys that the main characters take in the film 'Ladyhawke' and here we can see a number of character arcs that travel in tandem, within the overall story arc. The story arc is about the freeing of two lovers from a terrible curse, in order that they may be united again.

The character arcs reveal how each of the characters reaches that endpoint. By confronting their doubts and their fears and accepting love and trust to operate within their lives, the changes in their attitudes bring about their release. But each of them has varying degrees of reluctance, resistance to change and to trusting others.

Initially the primary journey is that of Etienne of Navarre {called Navarre in the film}. He is determined to kill the Bishop of Aquila but is prevented because he can only move as a man in daylight and the city is heavily guarded. We understand his pain and his need for revenge. We understand his longing for a love that has been denied him, by the Bishop's curse.

When the bells ring out telling of an escape from the dungeons, {up until now an unthinkable possibility} he knows his prayers have been answered. Although Navarre's character arc is the driving force of the narrative, his is not the principle character arc. That belongs to Philippe, right from the start it is his story.

Philippe 'The Mouse' is equal parts thief, liar, coward, companion, confidante and finally reluctant but courageous hero. A clever, deceitful adolescent who has no loyalties, except to himself. But he grows to love Isabeau the *'Ladyhawke'* of the title and commits to their salvation. There are three trials that Philippe must face once he has entered the Quest and here we see the power of Magic Numbers.

The first begins after he has taken the injured hawk to the monk Imperius, this being the moment when he is truly committed. In this first trial, he saves Isabeau on the edge of a tower, whilst being threatened by the Bishop's soldiers, at the moment when darkness turns to dawn.

The second requires him to save the wolf from a collapsing frozen river, a trial that almost costs him his life and in which he is physically scarred.

The third and final trial has him returning to the prison/citadel, where if he is caught he will be executed. Each of these episodes is more dangerous and challenging than the last.

Isabeau's character arc is similar to that of Navarre. She is wary of Philippe's motives, especially since he tricked her into freeing him, in the early part of their journey. But having saved her, at great risk to himself, she is willing in the end, to place her fate in his hands.

For Imperius, the guilt-ridden priest-confessor, this journey becomes one of redemption. He, with the aid of Philippe, has the chance to break the curse and make amends.

CHARACTER FLAWS

Why is the hero of the narrative Philippe?

A comparative look at the classic hero and the reluctant, flawed hero in 'Ladyhawke'

Our story opens with the escape of Philippe 'The Mouse' and shows only brief glimpses of the black knight Navarre. So clearly this is Philippe's story. He is a thief and extraordinarily dishonest, who even dares to bluff God about his misdeeds. Though Navarre intercedes and saves Philippe's life we see all that follows from Philippe's perspective, if not directly through his eyes. And yet he is not the traditional hero- Navarre is far more the hero/warrior in demeanour and appearance. A deliberate choice has been made here. {See **Catalyst Hero**}

The story could have begun with Navarre hearing the bells of the prison- citadel peeling and then seeking out why.

Hearing from a passer-by that someone has escaped, he enlists the escapee in his quest to kill the bishop.

As short-sighted and vengeful as it is – IT IS NAVARRE WHO HAS THE QUEST. He appears to be positioned as the traditional hero of the tale.

But we are playing against type here and it is the truly flawed character who will inherit the Quest on Navarre's behalf. Though powerful and determined, Navarre has little to gain in the story arc besides revenge. He does however learn humility and acceptance, which completes his character arc. He learns to trust and places his fate in the hands of Philippe and Imperius. Philippe is the reluctant hero. Initially he tries to disentangle himself from Navarre's vendetta.

'In truth, I have no honour and never will have.'

Philippe has a great deal to learn and it will cost him dearly. Navarre exists as a catalyst for Philippe's changes. Eventually Philippe will overcome his fears and reluctance and do such deeds as will bring him unexpected honour.

Choosing flawed characters creates the potential for deeper and richer characters. It gives them further to travel emotionally, psychologically and spiritually. They are far more interesting when played against type and expectation.

OH, AND ONE MORE THING

Taking the Hero's Journey to other genres

In this section of the book we have dealt almost exclusively with Fantasy Fiction and the Hero's Journey but this kind of blueprint can be adapted to write many kinds of stories. The journey of a hero through life's tribulations and dangers can be used in a novel built around an emotional journey, a portrait of self-discovery, a tale set in a war-torn land, historical fiction, crime novels or romance fiction to suggest only some of the genres.

The Hero's Journey works because it is our journey through life magnified. Each character faces trials and dangers that are true to human existence, the difference here being that they are set in more exotic landscapes and wear more gaudy apparel; admittedly with a little more of the supernatural thrown in.

In 'Realist Fiction' we can face questions of life and death, be guided by wise teachers and be aided by committed companions. We can face dangers that threaten our existence and we can draw upon all the skills and knowledge that a fantasy fiction character does to meet our challenges, barring magic.

Below is a list of novels that use the Hero's Journey schema but are more realistic in focus.

There are even more suggestions in the Recommended Reading and Viewing Lists.

Here are a number of Hero's Journeys within Classic and Modern Fiction'.

The Call of the Wild – Jack London
Moby Dick – Herman Melville
The Last of the Mohicans – James Fennimore Cooper
The Wild Girl - Kate Forsyth
Looking for Alaska – John Green
Enigma - Robert Harris
Pompeii – Robert Harris

POSTFACE

Before putting together WRITER, I taught storytelling and creative imagining in drama forms, for more than thirty years.

I both attended and ran creative writing workshops for twenty of those thirty years. In this book, I have attempted to give as thorough an overview of creative writing as possible.

I have done what all teachers worthy of the name have done, presenting 'the age old method of teaching' - THEORY, PROCESS, EXAMPLES, EXERCISES. This four-step procedure is how most subjects are taught.

It begins by showing you the **theory** behind stories and the **process** that writers often use to create. It then gives **examples** and asks you to create something new through **exercises**. Whether you are learning ballet, guitar, tennis or whatever, this is the tried and true method for acquiring a skill.

WHAT YOU SHOULD DO NEXT

Once you have the **theory** in your head you can and should investigate it far more thoroughly, going deeper and wider into the traditions and psychological insights inherent in the Hero's Journey and the theories covered in Writer 1.

You can discover other **processes** for writing, for there are always other processes. A good writer is always on the lookout for these. This book because of its' scope does not go into aspects of writing as deeply as books devoted to specific areas, such as plot, character or dialogue. Seek out these books and deepen your knowledge. Please use my Recommended Resources as a starting point. To be a great writer you need a wealth of knowledge and have read vast amounts.

Examples, of course, are numerous and offer you a lifetime of reading pleasure. You need to be as well read as possibly.

Finally, the **exercises** are up to you. There are 32 within this book but that is only the start. Others writers and workshops will offer you many more techniques. Finally, there is the work you do yourself over decades that will improve and refine your knowledge and your style.

Your writing might begin with a descriptive passage, a brief character study then to an anecdote, on to a short story and progress to novellas and novels and who knows maybe great sagas. Whatever you write the important thing is to write everyday

AND LASTLY.....

FORM NOT FORMULA

In these Ancient Tales lie the Stories of the Future

What we have explored in both mainstream and fantasy fiction has been presented in its most skeletal form. The challenge is to take these component parts and create new variations on the form. It is easy to see stories broken down into conventions, repeated arrangements and familiar styles.

But we all want much more than that. Take the building blocks here and rearrange them to **create something wonderfully new.**

I began this writing with an observation about The Beatles and their reworking of American Rhythm and Blues. They produced, out of a 12 note scale in 3/4. or 4/4 time several hundred songs, many of which went to places no-one had been. They saw, in a simple musical form and the experiences of their lives and imaginations, a chance to create music that was familiar and yet different to anything that went before.

As a writer, you should aim for the same level of originality and innovation.

Good Luck. You have begun your own Hero's Journey.
Luca Collins

APPENDIX

GARK'S STORY LOGIC FLAW

We have a group of hunters on the plains of Africa where abundant herds of grass eaters roam and yet these men are hunting a ferocious meat eater. Why would you do that?

The answer could have been provided as a narrative explanation by Gark to Sarz or it could have been part of the morning address to the troops by Rak.

The answer is that the 'Tiger' is their tribal totem and once every twelve moons they must prove their worth and hunt the tiger or else the hunting they do for the rest of the year will fail. It is their sacrifice to the Gods - either a hunter or a tiger.

Why did I not include this? The answer is it would have slowed the narrative down. Did anyone notice till I pointed out there was a flaw? Writers make decisions like this all the time.

APPENDIX

NAZI IDEOLOGY AND THE HERO'S JOURNEY

Even the best of things in this world can be corrupted by those with the intent. German folklore has a great many legends and folktales centred on noble knights and quests {The Seigfreid Saga}. The storylines and iconography of these were hijacked by the Third Reich in the 20s, 30s and 40s.

Hitler and his party used these symbols to help create an ideology that allowed them to justify the killing of millions and the extermination of the disabled, sexually different, gypsies and Jews.

Understandably in Germany, there has been reluctance by some to embrace the concepts of the Hero's Journey, as they have been so misused, in the 20th Century, by Germany's leaders during those dark times.

RECOMMENDED RESOURCES

PUBLICATIONS

All the books suggested are either vital or at least worthwhile. But the first books cited stand above all the others, for their insight into the story process and the hero's journey.

The Hero with a Thousand Faces - Joseph Campbell Pub. New World Library

The Writer's Journey – Christopher Vogler Pub. Michael Wiese Productions

Story – Robert McKee Pub. Methuen 1999

Writers' and Artists' Guide to How to Write - Harry Bingham Pub. Bloomsbury

Plot versus Character – Jeff Gerke Pub. Writer's Digest Books

OTHER RECOMMENDED TEXTS

Merriam-Webster's Concise Handbook for Writers -Pub.Merriam- Webster 1998 [All the grammar facts you need]

How to Read Literature Like a Professor – Thomas C. Foster Pub. Harper 2003

Understanding Novels – Thomas C. Foster Pub. A & c Black 2009

[Both books look at what books say and how readers read them]

Becoming a Writer- Dorothea Brande Pub. Tarcher/Putnam 1934

[A classic. Deals with confidence and application]

The Writers' and Artists' Yearbook – Pub. A & C Black 2005

[Information about the industry, copyright, approaching publishers. Updated regularly]

Becoming a Writer -Laurel Dumbrell Pub. Unwin Paperbacks 1986

[Methods and approaches. Very practical]

How Fiction Works- James Wood Pub. Vintage 2009

[Brilliant. Deals in detail with Realism then how consciousness/psychology has altered the novel]

The Story of the Novel – George Watson Pub Macmillan 1979

[A broad non-chronological history of the development of narrative and the novel]

The Art of Fiction – John Gardner Pub. Vintage 1991

[Great book especially plotting, P.O.V. Raymond Carver's teacher]

The Politics of Myth- Stephen Knight Pub. Melbourne University Press 2015

[Mythic figures both real and imagined. Analysis of power, resistance and knowledge through mythic icons.]

Abbey Lubbers, Banshees & Boggarts – *A Who's Who of Fairies* -Katharine Briggs Pub. Penguin 1979

No Go the Bogeyman – Marina Warner Pub. Vintage 1998

From the Beast to the Blonde – Marina Warner Vintage 1995

[All three books above – scholarly, amazing look at folktale history and origins]

1001Books You must Read before You Die – Ed, Peter Boxall Pub.Harper Collins 2012

101Books to Read before You Grow Up- Bianca Schulze Pub. Quarto 2016

[Both books above for widening and deepening your knowledge]

Big Magic- Creative Living without Fear - Elizabeth Gilbert   Bloomsbury 2015

[An insightful look at the nature of creativity. How artists inhibit themselves and how to break free]

READING LIST

Jane Austen

Sense and Sensibility

Phil Beadle

Dancing about Architecture

Robert Bloch

That Hell Bound Train

Ray Bradbury

Something Wicked This Way Comes

Dandelion Wine

Emily Bronte

Wuthering Heights

Charlotte Bronte

Jane Eyre

Italo Calvino

If On A Winter's Night A Traveller

Albert Camus

L'Etranger [The Stranger]

Angela Carter

The Bloody Chamber

Raymond Carver

Will You Please Be Quiet, Please?

Cervantes

Don Quixote

Raymond Chandler

The Big Sleep

The Maltese Falcon

Geoffrey Chaucer

The Canterbury Tales

Sir Arthur Conan Doyle

The Adventures of Sherlock Holmes

Joseph Conrad

Heart of Darkness

James Fennimore Cooper

The Last of the Mohicans

Susan Cooper

The Dark is Rising Sequence

Charles Dickens

A Tale of Two Cities

David Copperfield

Oliver Twist

Bleak House

Roald Dahl

The Witches

James and the Giant Peach

Daniel Defoe

Robinson Crusoe

Guy de Maupassant

A Day in the Country and other stories

Daphne du Maurier

Rebecca

F. Scott Fitzgerald

The Great Gatsby

Gustave Flaubert

Madame Bovary

Kate Forsyth

Bitter Greens

The Wild Girl

John Fowles

The Magus

Kenneth Grahame

Wind in the Willows

John Green

Looking for Alaska

Jakob and Wilhelm Grimm

Grimm's Fairytales

Robert Harris

Enigma

Fatherland

Pompei

Nathaniel Hawthorne

The Scarlet Letter

Ernest Hemingway

The Old Man and the Sea

O. Henry

The Four Million

Frank Herbert

Dune and Dune Messiah

William Horwood

The Willows in Winter

Duncton Wood

Thomas Hughes

Tom Brown's School Days

Aldous Huxley

Brave New World

Island

Henry James

The Turn of The Screw

Franz Kafka

Metamorphosis

The Trial

Thomas Keneally

Schindler's Ark

Daniel Keyes

Flowers for Algernon

Stephen King

The Dead Zone

Harper Lee

To Kill a Mockingbird

Laurie Lee

Cider with Rosie

Jack London

The Call of the Wild

Christopher Marlowe

Dr Faustus

Yann Martel

Life of Pi

George R.R. Martin

Songs of Fire and Ice

Hermann Melville

Moby Dick

Margaret Mitchell

Gone with the Wind

George Orwell

1984

Animal Farm

Katherine Paterson

The Bridge to Terabithia

Charles Perrault

Fairytales

Edgar Allen Poe

Tales of Mystery and Imagination

Anne Rice

Interview with the Vampire

J K Rowling

The Harry Potter Series

James Roy

Town

Sir Walter Scott

Ivanhoe

William Shakespeare

Macbeth

Midsummer Night's Dream

The Tempest

Romeo and Juliet

Twelfth Night

Mary Wollstonecraft Shelley

Frankenstein

John Steinbeck

Of Mice and Men

The Grapes of Wrath

Bram Stoker

Dracula

Jonathan Swift

Gulliver's Travels

J.R.R. Tolkien

The Lord of the Rings

The Hobbit

Mark Twain

Tom Sawyer Abroad

Huckleberry Finn

The Prince and the Pauper

H.G. Wells

War of the Worlds

Time Machine

Tim Winton

Breath

Dirt Music

John Wyndham

The Chrysalids

Unknown

Beowulf

Greek Myths and Legends including King Midas

Norse Myths

FILM

A Tale of Two Cities – Starring Dirk Bogarde U.K. [1958]

Ladyhawke – Richard Donner

Henry V – Director: Kenneth Branagh – Renaissance Films

Mary Shelley's Frankenstein - Director: Kenneth Branagh

The Harry Potter Films – Various Directors Warner Bros

WEBSITES

The Hero's Journey
http://www.mythichero.com/what_is_mythology.htm

Monomyth
http://orias.berkeley.edu/hero

The Monomyth Cycle
http://www.wiu.edu/users/mudjs1/monomyth.htm

Heroes of History
http://library.thinkquest.org/05aug/00212/monomyth.html

Bill Moyers on Faith and Reason
http://www.pbs.org/moyers/faithandreason/perspectives1.htm

www.ingramcontent.com/pod-product-compliance
Lightning Source LLC
Chambersburg PA
CBHW021053080526
44587CB00010B/233